Contents

Acknowledgments

Grateful acknowledgment is made to the following publications in which the poems in this book were originally printed:

AGNI: "Eating a Toad"

American Poetry Review: "In a Landfill," "In a Storm," "The Detective," "My Father Eating Ice Cream," "The Old Man of the Woods," "Epithalamion"

The American Scholar: "Bad"

Atlantic Monthly: "Crossing the Divide"

Canary River Review: "The Secret Agent"

Columbia Journal: "That Hunter"

Crazy Horse: "Audience," "The Message," "Nick," "In the Penny Arcade"

88: "On Being Asked to Discuss Poetic Theory," "Good Night," "In the Fog," "In Praise of the High Viscosity of the English Language"

Georgia Review: "The Bean Sprout"

Gettysburg Review: "Turning Over an Old Leaf," "Sleeping Alone," "A Report on the Excavation"

The Hampden-Sydney Review: "Floating"

Hanging Loose: "Trying to Make Music," "Introduction to a Poetry Reading," "A Woman in a Car Full of Flowers"

Hotel Amerika: "Pablo Neruda Catches the Rain"

Hudson Review: "A Falling Tree," "The Lookout," "Trying to Fall Asleep Beside an Iguana," "The Guide," "Homeowner"

Indiana Review: "Whistling"

The Kenyon Review: "Visiting the Lady with the Plant"

The Literary Review: "Bedtime," "Have You Any Questions About Your Garden?"

Manhattan Review: "How to Meet Strange Women," "Three Sketches in Watercolor"

Margie: "A Commencement Address (Short Version)," "At Lunch with the Psychiatrists," "At the Edge of a Clear-cut Forest," "Keep Out, Tresspassers Will Be Jailed After They Get Out of the Hospitle, This Means You!" "The Getaway," "The Three Monkeys," "At the Mirror"

New Letters: "Trying to Help a Stranger," "Moon Dance"

The New Republic: "Mr. Emerson Tries to Complete an Essay," "What to Do When Surrounded"

Northwest Review: "The Son of a Carpenter"

Ontario Review: "Instructions for Whistling in the Dark," "Arranging a Book of Poems"

Pleiades: "Big Game"

Poet Lore: "An Entomologist's Memo to Death," "Burnt Offering," "Invitation at the Edge of a Desert"

Poetry: "In Rubble," "The Fire-bringers," "Madman," "At the Foot of a Mountain," "The Good Night and Good Morning of Federico Garcia Lorca," "Curtains," "For a Man Dancing by Himself in a Tavern," "For a Student Sleeping in a Poetry Workshop," "Wanted," "The Models"

Poetry Miscellany: "Being a Model," "The Cold Doctor"

Shenandoah: "The Tree House," "Evening Song on Our Street," "Climbing a Tree"

Southern Review: "Hooverville," "The Magician," "Breakfast," "The Pickpocket"

Sou'wester: "Pressing Leaves," "The Kidnapper," "Self-portrait Ending with a Found Poem from *Life Histories of North American Birds*"

Threepenny Review: "Bad Chairs," "Snakeskin"

Western Humanities Review: "Under All Speech"

Witness: "Rooster," "For a Newborn Muskrat," "The Toad," "Lunch," "For an Old Woman Singing in the House Across the Street"

The Yale Review: "Sleeping in a Ditch," "Rehearsing the Death Scene"

I

The Good Night and Good Morning
of Federico Garcia Lorca

He knew he was asleep and was dreaming
    Of a beautiful poem. It seemed to be singing
        Itself in the night, and he woke
In a bed in a room in an old hotel
    And lay there, hearing the song go on
        Though he could see the shape
Of his empty shirt on the straight chair
    And his empty shoes on the patch of carpet
        Made light, half by the moon
And half by the gray beginning
    Of dawn. He could see the silhouette
        Of his own hand against the window shade
Like a flower, open and waiting. He smiled
    At the foolishness of loving his own poem
        In his own dream, of accepting praise
From his own shadow. But his mind's eye
    Kept seeing that poem and his real ear
        Kept hearing that same song. It came from the street
Under his window, and before he knew why,
    He was out of bed and shivering his way
        Clumsily into some of his old clothes
And one of his shoes and stumbling
    Into the hall and down the unlighted stairs
        And through the lobby (where the clerk was dreaming
Something else), through the stubbornly locked door
    And along the sidewalk to the curb where the singer
        Was sweeping trash and leaves along the gutter
With his slow broom, who now stopped, his mouth
    Open to gape at an apparition
        Holding a scrap of paper up to his face

And begging him to read aloud. The sweeper
   Whispered he couldn't read. And Lorca took him
      Into his arms and kissed him and kissed
The morning air, now stirring what was left
   Of the leaves overhead, and went limping back
      Through a door that stood wide open
And a grand lobby and up the stairs into bed
   To lie there stark awake as sleeplessly
      As a poet who'd been told he was immortal.

Evening Song on Our Street

It was almost bedtime, and something was wrong
On our street. We heard the sirens
And saw the lights, and my mother and father
Took me by my hands and walked with me

Over the tilted slabs of the slate sidewalk,
Under the branches of horse chestnut trees
To the wide lawn where people were being carried
Or half-carried in the near-darkness

Out of cars and flat-bed trucks and helped to lie down
On their own shadows, on folding cots or blankets
Or on bare grass because there were too many
To fit inside the rooms of the hospital.

The people were black and had eaten the wrong supper
While celebrating something, a man told us.
They were moaning and groaning to themselves, and some
Were humming out loud together, to each other,

And some were crying, and men in white coats
And women in white dresses and white hats
Were looking after them. They sounded like
People who had to sing, but were trying not to.

They sounded like they couldn't remember the words
But were singing anyway because they couldn't
Help it and because it made them feel better.
They had something inside they had to get rid of

Before it was too late, and they didn't care
If it was ugly or hard to listen to, they were going
To do it, and when the policeman told us
To keep out of the way because there was nothing

Practical we could do and that everything
Would be all right before long if we let nature
Take its course, my mother and father held me
By both my hands again, and we walked home.

Visiting the Lady with the Plant

It was almost going to be too late for me
    To go along because there were shadows
        Under the buckeye trees along our street,
But the lady with the plant had called my mother
    And father to come and see it blooming,
        So we walked and walked to that gray house
And up the steps and through the half-open door
    Where the lady in gray was sitting in a chair
        With wheels. It was darker than the beginning
Of the night outside. We moved our feet
    And our wheels on a soft carpet across a room
        Where the furniture was huddling under sheets
To another room. The walls and even the ceiling
    Were square pieces of window. I could see trees
        And other people's houses through them
In what was left of sunset. Then we all gathered
    Around the plant coming up out of real dirt.
        It was taller than my father. It was almost
Reaching the underside of the glass. Its leaves
    Had little jaggers along the edges and needles
        At the ends and long spikes of flowers,
Yellow-green and glowing. The lady said nobody
    Could tell ahead of time. You had to wait
        And maybe you couldn't
Wait long enough. You might die
    And never see it. And there it was
        Right in front of us, doing it just this once
In a hundred years. It would die now. My mother said
    It was beautiful, and my father and I
        Kept quiet, and all of us

Stood there a while, keeping quiet
   And behaving ourselves, not fidgeting,
      And then we said goodnight and went walking
Slowly and carefully home on slate and bricks
   And cobblestones, holding each other's hands
      Under the dim streetlights
And up more stairs into bed where we were all
   Supposed to be and going to be
      Good and think about it.

The Cold Doctor

In the first heavy winter of the Depression
His wife died, and the old doctor next door
Turned cold. He began gathering firewood
In his tall quiet house. A delivery truck
Would bring him cord after cord. And week after week
He carried it by the armload up his back steps
And through his kitchen door and out of sight
All spring and summer. Gradually the windows
Of the upstairs bedrooms filled with the seasoned ends
Of quartered cottonwood. By late September
He'd run out of rooms up there and began stacking
The dining room and the parlor and the pantry
And maybe the halls and closets we couldn't see
Because there was nowhere left on the outside
Where kids could stand on somebody else's back
And peek. We wondered: had his hair turned white
And his shoulders round inside his overcoat
Because he slept in the bathtub? There was no bed
In his tiny office, only a roll-top desk
And chair and an empty fireplace and a stool
Where my mother made me sit so I wouldn't die
Covered with spots. He scratched my shivery arm
With a needle that shook in his cold fingertips
While he smiled at me and told me to bundle up.

The Message

Something was in the sky. It was even bigger
Than our house and painted gray, and people were running
Along our alley to see it and pointing at it,
And all our neighbors were in their yards like me,
And the firemen had all come running out of their station,
And all the teachers and children at the school
Were out as if for recess, and it was flying
Lower and lower over the hospital,
And the sick people and nurses with white hats
Were standing out on the lawn. It was so big,
I couldn't understand how it could float
And turn and come still lower and closer,
And there was a man in a cabin under it
Who was leaning out of a window, waving at me,
And my father was beside me, waving back,
And knew the man's name. He hadn't always been
Up there. He'd gone to work where my father went
Almost every morning. Suddenly something
Was falling and glittering like pieces of tinfoil,
And one was white and quicker. It fell on our grass.
I picked it up and opened the crumpled paper
From around a stone. My father could read it
And even I could read it. It said my name.

Curtains

Grandpa took me along to the hospital
To help him hang new curtains in room after room
Where sick people in bed were going to be
Much better before long. He had to measure

How high and wide the windows were with a tape.
I got to climb a ladder and hold one end
And tell him the right numbers and sometimes
I was the one who wrote them down on a pad.

Some of the people wanted to know my name
And would ask how old I was and say *Oh my!*
Or *Imagine that!* or *Aren't you proud of him?*
To Grandpa, who said nothing but numbers

Because we still had so many rooms to go.
He was tall and gray and bent. His eyes, between eyelids
And eyelashes through his horn-rimmed spectacles
From under his dark eyebrows, measured me.

He was in dry goods. His Ideal Company
Was three floors high with little cars on wires
That ran through floors and ceilings from registers
Toward Grandpa behind glass. I tried to smile

At all the sick people, even the ones who said
They didn't want new curtains or anything else
But peace and quiet. And one man didn't want Grandpa
Covering his windows. He wanted to go on

Seeing God's Outdoors. And he didn't want me
Touching his magazines and looking at him.
Grandpa said he was going to put up curtains
Like it or not because it was his job

And the man should keep a civil tongue in his head
And use it to mind his manners with God indoors
And I should act my age and wait outside
In the corridor where somebody passed by

Under a sheet, who wasn't going to get better.
He was lying on a narrow table with wheels
Behind a blue-and-white nurse who smiled my way
And asked if I'd like to come along for a ride.

In the Penny Arcade, 1931

At the top of that machine
  When I let my pennies go
    Through a slot they went falling
Of their own weight along
  A vertical maze this way
    And that through a thicket
Of brass nails past my nose
  Against the blurry glass
    By the numbers that showed how
Fast they might multiply
  If only they took the right
    Crooked paths to the end
Where I would have nothing left
  To show for them or to show
    My father how little
I'd made of them after
  He'd let them drop
    Reluctantly one by one
Into my cupped hands
  Almost as carefully
    As they'd been dropped into his
From somewhere above us both
  In those hard times and now
    Were neither his nor mine.

The Bean Sprouts

First we put dirt into the skinny box
    The way the teacher said. That part was easy.
        I knew all about dirt
Already. And then we planted our beans,
    Three of them, here and here and here,
        And poked them an inch deep and watered them
And waited so many days, I could hardly remember
    What was under there. When crackly humps
        Appeared above two pale green things
Hunching themselves up and out between
    One Friday and one Monday, I watched closely
        All that week as the sprouts straightened
And the soaked and puckery skins of two of them
    Split, and the green gates of the cotyledons
        And the smaller, greener wings of the embryos
The teacher made us spell in our notebooks
    Opened as if to fly, but all the next week
        They didn't. The gates shrank, and the other wings
Spread wider, and one of them wider and wider
    Till it grew a shoot that pointed out of its middle
        Straight up, then curved and branched with a pair of sheaths
That looked like bean pods. Both the wings of the other
    Turned yellow and fell off, and the sprout curled
        And shrank back to the dirt. The third place,
Where the third bean was, didn't do anything.
    The one that was still alive climbed to the sill
        Of the middle window, with a little help
From string and thumbtacks, almost into the light
    Before our school was over and out. We were graded
        On spelling and organization

And neatness when we wrote about what had happened
    And what we'd done, but no one told us
        What to do about death and death and death.

The Toad

Where I grew up, the soil
Was sand, cinders, and slag
Dumped by refineries
And mills and open hearths
And foundries, spread around
And floated on a swamp
Till on good days and nights
It was almost real estate.

Plants grew as cautiously
And slowly as I did
Playing in vacant lots,
Sometimes digging holes
For treasure, but two feet down,
Finding the other side
Of the world ended in water
From the marsh across the road.

Once as I sat there thinking
As little as I could,
I saw a toad in the sedge
Beside me, near enough
To touch. In his wide mouth
The end of his hidden tongue
Waited for sundown.
Meanwhile, he was the shade
Of everything around him.

He had no jewel stuck
In his head. He wouldn't change
Overnight to something grand.

But he knew how to wait
(Long after wrens and herons
And mallards and mudhens
And the last of the muskrats
Had gone) for his mosquitoes,

The only others left
Alive to feed each other.
He watched as I caved in
The sides of my test hole
And muddled the crude oil,
Sulfuric acid, and rust,
And filled it and tamped it down
As hard as a founding father.

Hooverville

I wasn't supposed to go where the bums lived,
But I could see their houses made out of crates
And tin cans hammered flat, out of tarpaper
And cardboard boxes, the doorways curtained with rags.

I watched them wash their clothes and their underwear
And their bodies in cold Lake Michigan for a mile
Between us and South Chicago. Freight engineers
Would whistle and wave at me, but not at them.

My mother fed some almost every morning,
So I knew they'd ridden boxcars from somewhere else
And were going somewhere else sooner or later
But meanwhile had to stay here and be hungry.

I sneaked out of my bed and bedroom window
Some nights and saw their fires flicker to life
Along the tracks and burn from yellow to red
While a kind of hoe-down with banjos and guitars

Was creaking and plunking almost as faint and far
And near as the mosquitoes and hop toads
And crickets. I could hear them singing. Their shadows
Danced in firelight. Nobody danced in our yard

Or in our neighbors' yards. Our short front lawns
Ended in cindery ditches and roadbeds
Where cattails puffed their seeds over the cross-ties,
Where tumbleweeds, on the loose, were ready to roll.

Nick

Suddenly he'd be standing on the corner
In front of us, Nick Martich, who was twenty
Or thirty or forty, still wearing that shirt
(Out of somebody's ragbag or handed down
From the father we couldn't imagine) and those pants
(Pressed into permanent wrinkles by whatever
Had spilled on him lately) and those red suspenders
(Hiking him up high while he bobbed and weaved
Like a boxer). One arm was strong. It could make a fist.
It could straighten and point. It could shove itself
Into his pants pocket and dig down
For his latest news—a name, an address, a key,
Or half a candy bar—and the other was dead,
Boneless, almost elastic, with raw, red knuckles,
And he could swing it like a living whip
By swiveling his hips. It would sweep around
And slap his own back with a thud. Listen,
He'd knocked out so-and-so and so-and-so
Like that, and just like that, he would thump it
Against a telephone pole or a brick wall
And tell you to go ahead, smart-ass,
Stick a knife in it. With his good hand
He'd jam it into his pocket, take it out,
And jam it in again. He didn't have time
To stick around a bunch of fucking kids
Going to grade school who none of us didn't know
Which fucking end was up. He showed us a cundrum
And not no fucking balloon. We were too stupid
To know about cundrums or what they were for.
They were for fucking girls. We tried to imagine
What fucking girls were for as he limped away

To meet somebody important, his stiff back
Tilting and straightening, his curly hair
As tight as springs, his hare-lip puckered
To whistle us a song about what was up.

The Three Monkeys

They sat there on my bookshelf, my first prize
    From a carnival, three plaster monkeys
        In a row. My father said they were See and Hear
And Speak No Evil and said to think
    Of what those three were doing
        As a kind of Sunday school, and so
I started to think. The one with his hands
    Over his eyes like a blindfold
        Could say whatever he felt like
And could hear what anyone said and forget it
    Or remember. The one with his hands on his ears
        Had both eyes open
To everything going on and could say out loud
    Whatever he thought. The one clapping his mouth
        Shut could see and hear and keep in mind
Anything evil enough to reconsider
    Later, when those three, still stuck together
        But alone, could laugh and wave their hands in the air.

The Magician

In the tent at the carnival, the magician showed us
The woman's smiling head all by itself
In a box on a table with nothing under it
Except for the mirrors I knew all about.

I'd learned about all his tricks. I understood
How he linked and unlinked nickel-plated rings
And changed the colors of silk handkerchiefs
And made a dozen sponge-balls disappear

And reappear and multiply under cups.
I was an insider. I was fourteen.
I'd read all the books I could find about magic.
I'd practiced sleight-of-hand and fooled my friends.

The dozen other people who'd been wheedled
And barked inside the canvas weren't impressed.
They watched whatever he showed them sullenly
And didn't clap, then drifted back to the midway.

I stayed behind. He was making a cigarette
Disappear one puff at a time behind a flap
Where the woman's head was now wearing a torso
And drinking beer and looking tired of him.

I said I was a magician. Could I show him
What I could do? He shrugged. With my cold deck
I did arm-turnovers and accordion shuffles,
Back-palms, one-hand cuts, and waterfalls.

He didn't say anything. His thin mustache
Was blacker than licorice and twirled to points.
His cutaway had greasepaint on the lapels.
His clip-on bowtie had sprung his cardboard collar.

Her yellow sateen dressing gown and her shoes
And stockings looked as old as the Depression.
My shirt had once belonged to my big brother
When he'd been wider. My pants stopped short of my socks.

He said, *What do you really want to be?*
The woman laughed and spilled her beer in the sawdust.

My Father Eating Ice Cream

The handle of the spoon in all four fingers
    Of his right hand, up in tight
        Against the calluses, his wrist locked straight
In a line from second knuckles to elbow,
    His back not touching the chair-back but balanced
        Forward, his forearm level as a guard's
Brought up on offense, red in the face, perspiring,
    He would slide that baby,
        That sweetheart, into his mouth
As earnestly and thoughtfully as a paycheck
    Into a teller's cage. He was putting it where
        It would do the most good, and there would be more
Where that one came from, in a second service
    From one or another of the middle-aged
        Or young or old women who wore aprons
And understood how tall, how smooth the sides
    Of the mound melting in front of him should be,
        Whether he began at the pinnacle
Or was more inclined this evening to undermine
    And overtake upward, even with both his eyes
        Half closed, the slow descent
Of strawberries or raspberries, every one of which
    Would be caught up, rescued, and brought back,
        Just in time, to be put where it belonged.

The Guide

Visitor today: Professor David Wagoner
—from the bulletin board of McNeil Island
    Federal Penitentiary

My guide was an old marshal, lipless, thin,
    His face a permanent blush. He moved
        Deliberately at my side, slightly
Behind, never once touching
    My arm or pointing. He seemed to think
        I already knew where I was going
At least for two more hours. He showed me
    How to sit down in a cafeteria
        And eat without looking at anything
But a sandwich and, on the long way out,
    How not to listen to lip-smacks and wolf whistles
        From close behind. At each of the locked doors
Where we waited for a guard to remember us
    And let us go through, to make the latches
        Clank, he glanced at parts of my face
From under his porkpie hat and beyond my eyes
    Without quite meeting them. In the visitor's room
        He showed me the hard chairs and the glass wall,
Showed me the half-made bureaus and love-seats
    In the furniture shop and in the echoing cell-block
        Showed me two high tiers of empty cages
Facing each other. He told me, smiling,
    To stand on the spot where a prisoner had landed
        Smack on the concrete
From the top of the world and showed me a door with a window
    Where we could see the silhouette of a guard
        With a rifle in a tower, looking our way,

And said *he* could go out that door right now
    And walk along that path to the main gate
       And nothing at all would happen,
But if *I* should take it into my head to do likewise,
    That same guard would shoot me. He let me
        Think about that, then guided me down a ramp
And out to a dock where a boat was waiting
    And waiting to take some wives and me to the mainland.
      He said he hoped to see me again sometime.

Three Sketches in Watercolor

—for P.L.P.

1. *The House on the Sand*

It was their first idea: to build their house
On sand. It was beautiful there. They wanted to live
Among the dream-like dunes. They wanted to feel
Like shorebirds, to be as close to the weather
And the changes of the moon
As the sea would let them. But no matter how far
Down they drove the pilings, they disappeared,
And the foundation floated
Like a raft the rain and the prevailing wind
Kept testing, rippling and tilting their ways through
And under and around. When they'd first stood there
By the empty shore, admiring the mirage
Of their future view, why hadn't they looked down
At their feet, at their toes and arches
Going slipshod, while a breeze
And their own weight began to bury them?

2. *Walking Along the Shore*

Their feet came down on sand as gently
And deliberately as time and tide and their bodies
Allowed them to. When they looked back, they saw
The surf already smoothing every trace
Of where they'd been, receding, coming again
To falter and back away with its over-familiar
Dismissive gestures: they could have written their names
As often as footprints, but neither would have lasted
Long enough to remind them of the first

Impressions they made together, and wouldn't have been
More memorable, sad is to say, than a wave was.

3. *A View of the Shore from the Resort Hotel*

At dusk, when children, joggers, and racing dogs
Are no longer in the running, the young and old
Lovers and mixed singles go strolling along
The slightly canted shoreline where the sea
Is constantly making way for their bare feet.

They almost never turn landward or seaward.
Dry sand is too compelling and salt water
Too cold and too final. They want to walk ahead
Into the distance, though all of them must know,
As climbers know, they'll have to repay each step.

Alone or together, they dwindle into a wash
Of twilight and mist. Their figures in a seascape
Would take a skillful painter less than a moment—
A touch of a darker shade against the fading
Away of a predetermined vanishing point.

Keep Out, Tresspassers Will Be Jailed
After They Get Out of the Hospitle,
This Means You!

The sign had worked so far: no other cars
Had beaten the grass down between the ruts,
And no one had stomped a path through the knee-high lawn
Lately or walked the plank up to the porch
And pushed the door on its only hinge but you.

Whatever could be wrenched or crowbarred loose
Had been, including the kitchen sink, and the floor
Was hanging tough by its linoleum.
In the living room, someone had built a fire
For hotdogs or heat, but not in the fireplace.

The holes gouged in the wallboard between studs
Went all the way to the woods, the holes in the ceiling
Went all the way to the sky, and the three holes
In the bathroom floor were offering
Indoor plumbing direct to the foundation.

You inspected the scene of the crime. A few remains
Of the biggest, longest, maybe the worst party
Ever. Three sticks of furniture. The last dishrag.
A tag end of a nightgown. In the bedroom,
No telling where the Beautyrest had been

Or why. You found some overdue grocery bills
And receipts for speeding fines. A note saying, *Baby,*
Gone to the dump again. You went outside.
A swing-set with no swings. A slide with no ladder.
And what comes down the chimney? Half the chimney.

Along the side path, blossoming in the sun,
Bright, everlasting slivers of windowpanes.
A trellis where the rose hadn't been wild
Enough to keep from choking on itself.
A wooden pump-tower, knock-kneed, straddling a well.

Over the barn door, a rusty horseshoe
Wrong side down.
Inside, some shotgun shells and barn owl pellets,
But the owls themselves no longer living aloft.
Underfoot, not enough straw for a scarecrow.

In the back yard, a tipped-over lawn chair,
No grimier than your jeans. You sat in it,
Neck deep in wavering grass, drinking your lunch
To celebrate all this picturesque failure.
It made you feel irrationally happy.

Being nosy and on your own, you'd crossed the threshold
With the diffident easy bluster of a landlord
Or a crooked building inspector or a burglar
Professional to the core or a case-worker
With a warrant or a tour guide casing a ruin.

You felt so self-contained, so worldly (and you
Still middle-aged) to see these premises
Vacated like the premises you'd made
About a wife and hypothetical family
Once upon a time on a model farm,

You went to the country tavern at sundown
And, under the influence of a jukebox
And other brilliant conversationalists,
Joined some familiar strangers out for a night:
Jocose, Bellicose, Lachrymose, Comatose.

Home Owner

I had come back to a house I thought was mine,
Locked tight and almost paid for. It was empty
Except for a dog and Goodwill furniture,

But through the glass of the dead-bolted front door
Before I could turn the key, I saw a face
That wasn't supposed to be there. I'd seen it

Often, or ones like it, on street corners
When I would mutter, *No, I'm very sorry,*
No handouts before the hard-luck stories

Were halfway through. A black face. Young.
Now staring with black-and-white eyes from the inside
Like a home-owner surprised by a bill-collector.

He scrambled away out of sight toward what I'd thought
Was my kitchen. I ran around to the garden
To meet him (as he stumbled down the steps)

And wrestled him to the ground and held him there.
For whole seconds we had nothing to do
Or say. His eyes were shut. I looked at my lawn,

My garage, my fence, my roses, my cherry tree,
My birdbath. He was twelve. When I let him go,
He dove into weeds. I shut a broken window

And some open drawers like an inside man concealing
Evidence. Then I solved the Mystery
Of the Watchdog That Only Watched:

She was licking an empty bowl, which had been filled
By a wonderful stranger. She was dancing around me
And around me, hoping I'd be wonderful too.

Tree House

Last spring a neighbor boy
Nailed up a house in a tree
With a floor like a life-raft,
With kindling for a ladder,
And a sagging lean-to roof.
Inside, he hardly seemed
To move through summer sun
And wind, then rain and frost.

And once, after his mother
Had called and waited and called
And his father had yelled his first,
Middle, and last names
Before slamming the door,
He stayed there after sunset,
Turning dark, being overcast
By the shadows of the leaves

And becoming someone else
That wasn't a boy in a tree,
Not just a pair of eyes
Or a shape in a different stillness,
But something older, waiting
To be changed in a growing place
With only one way down
And with only one way in.

Climbing a Tree

My daughter's red-winged kite is stuck in the branches
    Of a maple tree almost as mature
        As I'm supposed to be,
And though I give her a choice
    Of another kite in the immediate future
        And even another tree to go with it,
She wants this one. So instead of staying
    Here and standing my ground, I begin climbing
        And eventually actually make it
To the first fork, where the tree itself
    Decided to double its chances of not toppling,
        And reconsider my position
Crotch to crotch with the home of our ancestors
    Who, at the edges of forests in the evening,
        After foraging the strange, wide-open savanna,
Returned to spend the night high among birds,
    The bird in this case being unable to fly
        Without us. We're having to leave it
Alone, to die alone. We're having to walk away
    Without it, despite her wailing, as the night
        Begins down here on dangerous grassland.

A Skating Lesson

Her mother has brought her halfway
    Along a slippery road, but today her father
        Is more or less standing
In at the outer edge
    Of the rink, and she's holding his hand
        And his forearm and wants to depend
On both of them whenever she lurches, whenever
    Her lovely gangly legs
        And unpredictable ankles
Go off on their own ways
    Involuntarily, but has learned
        Quickly the other lesson
For this morning: she's going to be almost
    On her own as they shuffle together
        Rigidly forward, their spare hands
Both reaching now for the uncertainty
    Of each other
        Or the railing in order to glide
Along with the sure-footed, sure-bladed,
    Embarrassingly good skaters
        Passing them by, and all the way
Around, she holds herself
    Erect, brave and frightened,
        And, having come full circle,
Turns and smiles at her lock-kneed, concerned,
    Suddenly no-longer-cold, shakily
        Upright, devoted pupil.

Pressing Leaves

My daughters bring me leaves
  From under bushes, from underfoot, from the gutter,
    The shapes and colors
Of the sweepings of the wind
  At the end of October. They love them. Oh,
    They don't want them to change,
To curl and fade, to shrink
  And crumble into hiding
    Underground somewhere. They want the gold
And crimson, the magenta and stark yellow
  And the nameless shades they've seen dwindle
    To lace, to nearly nothing
All to lie down now under their orders,
  Under the sheets of daily news
    And the firm, weighty, almost
Unabridged dictionary, which will be lifted
  Away once daily to let them breathe, to dry
    Even more completely, to stiffen
Into something not even they, with all their charms,
  Had dreamed of, to be pressed
    Once again till the dawn of the sixth day
Will bring them out to be named in memory
  Of their lost wild mothers and fathers
    And whole forests
Of branching family trees, to be held
  Up to the light and remembered and counted on
    To help the others unfold outside the window.

Breakfast

By the window, my girls are eating eggs and cereal
And reading out loud the riddles and the rules
On the back of the box. They want to enter the contest
And win something amazing. Across the street,
Half on the sidewalk and half in a driveway,
A pack of dogs surrounds a crouched, much smaller
Mammal of some kind, lunging and snapping at it,
And one part shepherd picks that bundle up
In a quick sweep of its jaws and slams it
Down on the curb in a flash of red, and a runt
Retriever trots away with it off screen.
The girls have answers to all their questions now
Except a hard one and want me to decide.

Lunch

In the open-ended stable, the sparrows and I
Were having lunch. Mine was spread out on slices
Of whole-grain bread, and theirs was the grain itself,
Left on the floor by horses in windfall apples.

Below their nests in the loft and out in the paddock
Where the grainy, recycled, thoroughly stomped mud
To them seemed one more part of the pecking order,
The birds were feeling at home, stoking their fires

For the downhill flight from noon to a good evening.
And so was I, when, quick, over my shoulder
One sparrow rocketed at a critical angle,
Half stalling, straining under the overhang,

And through a shaft of sunlight a sky-blue-pinioned
Midnight-helmeted sparrow hawk with a soundless
Swoop impaled him, and they hovered there
With the shock of opposite, unequal forces

(While the sparrow sang the only note he knew
For outrage or anything else like territory
Or hunger or love or death), and they flew away
Together to the crown of an ash tree.

Bedtime

These two girls are thinking
    Of almost everything
They can think of that doesn't go
    To bed right now. They've brushed
And washed as slowly
    As those two other girls
In the bathroom mirror
    Who are trying not to look
Sleepy either, who can hardly
    Hear what their names are
As they dawdle on bare feet
    To the edge of their mattresses
And pretend they've forgotten how
    To climb up and lie down,
And they aren't quite sure where
    They were, but they know the moment
Their ears are against those pillows
    They might give in and stay
There, though they won't be
    Who or what they want
To be, but will fall into place
    In a story where everyone
Is asleep and will never know
    When to remember why.

2

Introduction to a Poetry Reading

Others before me have stood up here alone
   On stages something like this
      And imitated birds with their bare lips,
And some have fashioned intricate shadows
   On a screen with their own two hands and some have sung
      And danced without even taking their clothes off
And managed to survive you. Unthal the Armless,
   The Pedal Paganini, could play the fiddle
      With his bare feet, and Leopoldo Fregoli,
The quickest of quick-change artists, accompanied
   Himself at the piano while he sang a solo
      On the far side of the stage in an evening gown,
And all the wizards have been here, the crystal gazers,
   Manipulators, mind-readers, Mr. Memory,
      Jugglers and calculators, and that French hero,
Joseph Pujol, the Fartomaniac,
   Who could reproduce the tearing of calico,
      Cannon fire, thunder, whistle "Au Claire de Lune,"
And blow out candles. And all the stand-up comics
   Have suffered your shrewd judgment. Most have been heckled
      From the cheap seats like the music-hall M.C.
Whose jokes fell flat, who heard the audience chanting
   "Sing us a song," who said he couldn't sing,
      Who heard the same voices shouting "Then
Show us your cock!" And so, in that wobbly line
   Of entertainers, who are almost all
      Grateful to be dead, I offer this bouquet
Of personally inspected, prearranged,
   Simple-seeming, marginally useful,
      Preservative-free, unscented, fresh-cut poems.

Arranging a Book of Poems

You've lined them all up artfully, but the browsers
Leafing ahead won't pay the price of attention
To your clowns and balloons, your wavering stilt walkers,
And may not pause to notice your elephants
Have caught each other's tails in their trunks to start
The big parade without them. You won't have a chance
To jam your mouth against a microphone
And mesmerize the imaginary crowd
In the bleachers beyond the rings and the sawdust
With your over-the-top rendition of some number
From the sure-fire songbook. You
With your master-of-ceremonies gloves
Off may have spent foul beautifully helpless
Days and days getting this show in line,
But their eyes and ears are only skimming
And half-catching the acts you counted on
For more than just smoke and spangles, spectacular
Booms in surprising places, animals
Retrained to seem much wilder than they were,
And superstar artistes risking their lives
On eyebolts, cranks, and guy wires rigged in the dark
By loaded roustabouts. You thought you might be
Giving them more than popcorn and Day-Glo
Sweetness and strobe light, more than whizzers
And sparkling suckers. Well, it could have been worse.
You could have arranged a slow small-town parade
So full of citizens and dignitaries
Carrying home-made banners, no one was left
On the sidewalks to watch and cheer, and there was nowhere
To lead the bad brass band but out of town.

Trying to Make Music

A poet is trying to make music
out of the tumult of the dictionary.
—Boris Pasternak

Getting the right words in the right order
    Is everyone's problem, but trying to make music
        At the same time (and often having to turn
And shut your mouth for a moment
    At the end of what you imagine is the end
        Of a line) is a poet's burden. All around you
And even inside your head the giggling and shouting
    Go on and on, the deliberate misquotations
        From someone you can't remember and don't want to,
And even if angels or that grizzly hag, your muse,
    Were to dictate directly, clearly *sotto voce*
        A perfect poem into your earhole,
The signature would seem wrong. The key would seem wrong.
    And along the mildewed corridors
        And high through the tiers of the echoing madhouse
You call your native tongue, you would hear
    The catcalls, the snide cackling, the whispering
        From cell to cell at the same time as the Voice
Of the loudspeaker is babbling something crucial
    And the chorus of tone-deaf guards is bellowing
        Lock-down and Body Search! Silence and Lights Out!

A Date with the Muse

I smile across the intimate table
    Where the waiter has laid the silver,
        The ingeniously folded napkins,
And the gleaming crystal,
    Where I've set the Tiffany gift-box
        To be opened later. She regards me
Remotely with the poise
    Of the queen of a distant country
        Expecting something bizarre
From a savage suitor. I tell her
    She's beautiful. She mutters, *That goes*
        Without saying. I ask her
Over the open menu whether
    Anything, anything at all tonight
        Seems tempting, and the dim
Romantic light grows dimmer
    As she answers listlessly
        She isn't hungry. Listen then
For a moment please to this music,
    I whisper. Shall we dance?
        She smiles vaguely and murmurs
No thank you, not this evening,
    And the space between us yawns
        As wide as the empty dance floor.

For a Student Sleeping in a Poetry Workshop

I've watched his eyelids sag, spring open
    Vaguely and gradually go sliding
        Shut again, fly up
With a kind of drunken surprise, then wobble
    Peacefully together to send him
        Home from one school early. Soon his lashes
Flutter in REM sleep. I suppose he's dreaming
    What all of us kings and poets and peasants
        Have dreamed: of not making the grade,
Of draining the inexhaustible horn cup
    Of the cerebral cortex where ganglions
        Are ganging up on us with more connections
Than atoms in heaven, but coming up once more
    Empty. I see a clear stillness
        Settle over his face, a calming of the surface
Of water when the wind dies. Somewhere
    Down there, he's taking another course
        Whose resonance (let's hope) resembles
The muttered thunder, the gutter bowling, the lightning
    Of minor minions of Thor, the groans and gurgling
        Of feral lovers and preliterate Mowglis, the songs
Of shamans whistled through bird bones. A worried neighbor
    Gives him the elbow, and he shudders
        Awake, recollects himself, brings back
His hands from aboriginal outposts,
    Takes in new light, reorganizes his shoes,
        Stands up in them at the buzzer, barely recalls
His books and notebooks, meets my eyes
    And wonders what to say and whether to say it,
        Then keeps it to himself as today's lesson.

Poetry in Motion

The dancer spins from point to point, and the halfback
    Threads his way through a broken field
        Untouched, and the power forward
Hangs in the air too long to be quite
    Human, and the weightless gymnast whirling
        Through an arc of her own invention falls
To a balanced standstill. The commentators
    Call them *Poetry in Motion* as if to say
        Poetry might be almost as wonderful
If only it could move like them, if only it could
    Swivel and pirouette, if only it knew how
        To carry itself at suddenly shifting speeds
Alone and upright in unexpected directions
    Among opponents, if only it could leap
        Into the air and linger
There, up there as lightly as if there were nothing
    On earth to be heavy about, if it could seem
        As buoyant and graceful
As the human body watched from a safe distance,
    If only it could move itself and more
        Than itself and not be here, flat on a page.

In Praise of the High Viscosity
of the English Language

Your sluggishness seems well worth
   Muddling in without
      A good excuse. A line
Slogging its short passage
   Through your quagmire
      Without losing both boots
And waddling off off
   Balance will find a better poem
      Than this one now and be
Slipperier at it. Oh, what
   Messes we've all made
      With all our slewfoot efforts
To clarify your nature and how
   Hard you've made it for us even
      To do this little. For sheer
Thickness, no pond bed
   Unsettled by cows wading
      Could ever match what some
Of us poor souls have gone on
   And on stirring up in you,
      Yet we'd have made and said
And done nothing by now
   And would have gone nowhere far
      Faster without you.

Under All Speech

Under all speech which is good for anything
lies a silence which is better.
—Thomas Carlyle

Under all your making of language, all your loud and soft, tedious and
      compelling persuasion, all your insistence, your dramatically
      punctuated, percussive, tip-of-the-tongue plosives and dentates,
Under all your flat-out demands, your take-it-or-leave-it, opinionated
      circumlocutions and tub-thumping bellows, all that beating
      about the bush like the signal-thumping of jack rabbits, that
      ponderous, plum-lipped, over-ripe plucking in the orchards of
      Webster and Euphues,
Above and beyond the calls of self-helpful twittering and gibberish
      and disinformative calculation, the conniving clucks and uh's
      and tch's and um's and smacks and the prolonged periods of the
      preposterously overfilled withholdings of common knowledge,
And far away under the fossils of the fleshpotted and hang-doggedly
      prettified, ugly, autodictatable, not even good-for-a-laugh
      throat-clearing blabber, sentenced to death with the rest of our
      lost baggage below the morass of the mumbles from beneath
      our diagrams and diaphragms,
There is a silence that is, no doubt, worth more
Than what the tourists in four loud indistinct
Languages are telling themselves this evening
As they chatter on Cheyne Walk where Carlyle strolled
And mused and chose the words he kept to himself
Till they seemed worthwhile by the rise and fall of the Thames.

On Being Asked to Discuss Poetic Theory

I know for a fact snow falls in the mountains.
　　I've stood there while it fell
　　　　On me and the temporarily bare stones.
I could see it falling into the broken baffles
　　Of granite, hovering on the edge
　　　　Of thawing or staying frozen, both joining
And withholding itself from its other self
　　At the confused beginning of spillways
　　　　And misdirected channels and transparently
Aimless pools while it gathered
　　And went less often in the wrong directions,
　　　　And I've followed the water down (like it, with no need
To remember where I was or what I was)
　　And stood beside its mouth on the ocean shore
　　　　And looked back at the source,
At that stark whiteness. If it all disappears
　　Behind clouds this winter, I can be certain
　　　　That where I climbed those steeper and steeper miles
Along its path to the end of trees, to the end
　　Of crouching shrubs, to the last of the tendrils
　　　　And wild flowerheads, the same snow is falling.

Mr. Emerson Tries to Complete an Essay

At his hard desk, no longer wholly conscious
  Of the pen in his right hand, no longer confined
    By the dimensions of the floor and the four walls
But ascending through the ceiling toward the threshold
  Of Transcendental Understanding, he heard
    Ker-luck-a-put, cluck, the chickens, his own
Chickens outside the window, one of which
  Would be reduced to portions of itself
    And stewed for dinner, and though he had lost
The thrust of his hierarchic argument
  For a moment, he took the chicken to be an example
    Of the universally disguised emblems
Of Earthly Duty, and when the door flew open
  To reveal the offerings, on one hand and the other,
    Of carpet samples, one dearer, one less lasting,
He took it as his share in the design
  Of the Awesome Now on which the gods themselves
    Would weave the threads of an instrumental order
From the Raw Mundane to the Ineffable,
  Both necessarily now being postponed
    For his best black mourning suit and a mourning band
Firmly clasped on his biceps and his hat
  Just as firmly set so the narrow brim
    Was central to the brow and the occiput
And crossed both temples equally on the way
  To the carriage, up the step to his plush cushion
    And the funeral of a newly translated cousin.

The Three Trolls of Henrik Ibsen

In the drawer of his work desk, Ibsen kept three trolls,
    Squat little dolls with pointed hats
        And heads, with gnarled faces
And rumpled clothes, wicked and powerful,
    Unhappy with themselves, but overjoyed
        Being disagreeable. When a difficult scene
Was lying flat on his page, when it blurred
    And came to a halt, the way a young hero might
        At a crossroads, unsure of himself, not knowing
Which voice in the back of his mind to follow,
    Ibsen would open that drawer, bring out a troll,
        And stand it upright by the right-hand margin
Where it would demand tribute from his pen
    As it faltered nearer and nearer, scratching,
        And his words would trick that troll, slip by,
And turn to the next line, trick it again, and keep inching
    Forward on the adventure. Sometimes ahead
        He would see actors gathered beyond the bridge
Where the rest of the story was, their mouths open
    But silent. They were waiting for him to tell them
        What to do with their bodies and halting tongues
Instead of disappearing. So out of the drawer
    Ibsen would bring the second troll, even uglier
        Than the first, a smaller, greedier misfit
Born to be deceived, to go stumbling backward
    Into the creek, to huddle in a culvert,
        Glum and humiliated, while the hero
And his friends went on to the end of the last page
    And the curtain. The third troll, the smallest, the darkest,
        Stayed there shut in his drawer till Ibsen died.

Pablo Neruda Catches the Rain

Each day the rain fell
Into his father's house
Through old nail holes
In the corrugated roof
From under and along the loose
Tilted iron sheets. The boy
Could hear it
Dropping in every room,
Even there by his desk
Where he was making
New forbidden poems
Out of old words. The rain
Was a strange piano
With nine white keys. Two
Were like old coins
Falling in tin cans. Three
In three glass bowls
Were like the weeping
Of laundry. One
In an enamel basin
Was like the pulsing thrum
Of a frog. One in the den
In a brass spittoon
Was like the hawked phlegm
Of a wizard. In the bedroom
The distillates of the night
Slurred in a chamber pot,
And the last by the back door
Was like the faint slow
Note of the last trump
In a bedpan. When he would hear

The moan of the night train
Bringing his father home,
He would empty all nine
Vessels full of songs
Like the nine long years
Of a lifetime, pouring them
Out the window, one by one.

3

The Models

Music begins, and here they come toward us,
Not walking or dancing along the ramp, but making
Angular progress with no destination
But our poor eyes, which they meet in vain in passing
But wouldn't dream of meeting twice, not even
Now or again as they turn and pause, then turn
Again and pause again while they lift open
And shut the bizarre, the seemingly freely floating
And seamless openings of those smooth trappings
Someone imagined they should hold above us
And loosen lightly and fling aside from their skins
And bones, then close too soon as we gape back
And forth and up to them, trying to think
Of anything else, since they don't eat or speak
A living tongue, don't drink because their fingers
Have never gathered together into hands
Like ours and would never feel a common need
To applaud or wash themselves and because those legs
Couldn't stand still in rooms with us or bend
To allow those torsos to sit down in rows
Like us to watch their perfect counterparts
Enter the only light. Now, just as we thought,
They turn and disappear behind curtains.

How to Meet Strange Women

To teach you to say out loud what you've been saying
    With your mouth shut in the corner of the party
        (That loveless nook where you've been keeping yourself
Company or somewhere out in the hallway
    With family photos and bric-a-brac), here we come
        To your rescue with our guide. If some small part
Of your mind or body registers an attraction
    For a strange woman, first, you stand nearby
        On both feet within arm's reach of her
And the hors d'oeuvres. You smile,
    Not showing your teeth. You say to her directly
        Into her face, *No, I don't think you can
Possibly be as hungry as I am.*
    You smile again. *Would you consider trying
        A little of this?* And you arrange one morsel
Of anything on a plate and offer it
    Ceremoniously. You say, *I'm tempted
        But can't decide whether it's good for me.
Make up my mind for me.* If she ignores you
    Or walks away, you're free to try another
        And another. These are the moments
When you will learn how strange some women are
    And perhaps how strange you are, how strange
        You were with your unnatural diffidence
(Inherited from unmentionable people)
    At all those social crossroads, unable to choose
        The right fork or the left, and when you've followed
This or some other of our simple routines
    And find yourself with her at the front door,
        Leading her fearlessly across the threshold

And down the steps to the sidewalk without stumbling,
You'll take her with you out into the night
For our next lesson at a surprising cost.

Rehearsing the Death Scene

The light man and the director are downstage
   Looking up and pointing and arguing
      About invisible shades. The leading lady
Is in the wings, being retouched. The old heavy
   Sits on the apron, telling the prop girl
      (In her left ear) news of a private matter,
And the tragedian is sprawled in the bed
   Left over from the comedy, muttering
      The speech that will leave him cold: his final words
(So hard to project when he's supposedly
   Breathing his last), then his business
      With the eyes, then nothing but the tableau
Of death in the middle of a scene when everyone else
   Will be running the gamut. And now the cold light man
      And the pale director have momentarily
Killed their shadows. The leading lady has held
   The mirror up to her nature. The heavy resumes
      His darker public self. The tragedian
(Who would die in every act if he could, who would die
   In the prologue and epilogue, who would go on
      And on and off dying encore after encore)
Props himself up in character, ready to be
   A straight man without straight lines, and his understudy
      Slumps in the front row, nibbling a hangnail.

For an Old Woman Singing in the House Across the Street

Framed by the half-drawn drapes, she holds herself
   Close with her elbows, her clenched fingers
      Under her chin, eyes shut, her mouth
Open against the silence which is all
   I can catch from this distance over here
      In a listening house. She's wearing
A floor-length pale-blue terry-cloth bathrobe
   With the panache of a designer's ad, her coiffure
      A swirl of lavender toweling. She must be singing
Something unpopular, something seriously
   Heartfelt from the beginning or the end
      Of another time. Now her mouth closes
To a deeply inward smile as if she's hearing
   Applause. She blinks at it. She glances
      Left and right to take in the surprise
Of all this fuss over after all what had been
   Only an impulse, a private performance
      Impromptu. Her fingertips trace lightly
The line of her jaw and touch the arch of her throat
   And pause. Shaking her head, she turns
      And sweeps the trailing edge of her robe aside
With the practiced ease of a diva
   About to make her way into the wings
      Over the patent-leather pumps of the concertmaster
And second violinists, and she's gone
   Offstage, returning almost at once, in her arms
      A load of laundry, the blossoms of flowered prints.

For a Man Dancing by Himself in a Tavern

In the hall between the Ladies' and Gentlemen's
The man in the overcoat with the lost lining
Has started dancing, slowly at first,
Lifting his sleeves with his arms, having almost nowhere
To put his brimful glass but his own lips,
But now he toasts the ceiling with one hand,
Presses his belly like the small of a back,

And waltzes to rock and roll, his tongueless shoes
Sliding on open tiptoes, dividing three
By four with abrupt rubatos, with dizzy changes
Of signature and runs of accidentals,
His face suffused with the gold light bathing him
By courtesy of the Miller Brewing Company,
His eyelids like shut petals of rosebuds.

He is so wonderfully and completely happy
Holding her in his arms, so sure of the pleasure
She takes in his sweet nothings, so unaware
Of the comings and goings of insignificant
Others, so filled with her, his follower,
His drinking partner lighter than Lite beer
And more fulfilling, what else could he wish for?

Revolving slowly like the overhead fans
And the room, and down and around to a bent knee,
He doffs his baseball cap to the wallflowers
And shakes hands with himself. His hands shaking,
He takes himself by the elbows. The bartender
Takes him too, still bowing and still glowing,
Toward the door and out into the dark.

Bad

for Carolyn Kizer
who once told me this story

She had been bad, very bad at dinner, and was told
   If she didn't stop being bad
      Downstairs, she would have to go upstairs
And be bad all by herself, and if she didn't
   Concentrate right now on the idea
      Of being good, the Devil would come
And get her. But she went right on
   Being bad and wouldn't go up
      When she was told and finally
Had to be scolded and carried up the stairs
   And put to bed bad
      And told to think under the covers
Very carefully about her behavior
   With her head on a strange pillow
      And act her age. And her mother went downstairs
To her relatives who all agreed
   To go on fortifying their positions
      With the elixirs of mountain monks, the calming
Essences of a suddenly more
   Reasonable evening. But soon they could hear
      A murmuring from above like the spell
Of an enchanted princess saying something or other
   Over and over. The tight-lipped mother
      Stalked upstairs, intending to call that child
To order, but outside the bedroom door
   She heard the high voice crooning steadily
      And soothingly, *Go away, Devil,*
Go away, Devil, go away,
   Devil, and that mother felt a flurry
      Of remorse and entered and found her daughter

Sitting up in a strange bed as rigid
     As a new pupil, staring toward the window
          Open to good fresh air, beyond the antique
Cherry footboard where the great horned owl,
     His head swiveling slightly to comprehend,
          Had perched to listen with his whole attention.

Whistling

The boy had been left alone all afternoon
In that house at the edge of the woods. He'd played old games
By himself, he'd talked to himself, he'd sung old songs
To himself, and late in the day, he found a whistle
In his father's backpack and took it along outdoors
And made it whistle while he walked by himself
To the end of the pasture fence. If he blew hard,
The sound was almost higher than he could hear.
If he barely breathed in it, it made him feel
Like a small owl. If he blew harder, he imagined
The sky-high red-tailed hawk crying out again
At the sight of him by the lake. If he blew even
Harder than that, he could hear the rabbit singing
The only song it knew, the only notes
It had time to remember before the coyote
Carried it out of hearing. The boy sat down
And whistled high and low in the fading light
And closed his eyes by himself and opened them
(He thought) by himself, and he was staring
Into the greenish-yellow irises
And upright pupils (near enough to touch)
Of a wildcat listening, wondering what he was.

Bad Chairs

Some have secret sorrows. They hold nothing
    Against you personally,
        But their lack of pleasure
In themselves is so deep-seated,
    They pay little attention to posturing
        On your part. Some of them go
Into retreat at the slightest hint
    Of pressure from above
        And act imposed on
When you try to follow them
    Down to their own level
        With that sinking feeling. Others
May offer uncompromising support
    Of your unofficial position
        From the git-go, showing you how
To straighten up, so you won't be
    Wasting any more time
        Sitting down on the job. They want you
Never to swivel, never to bend over
    Backwards, but to stand up
        For yourself on your own four legs.

At Lunch with the Psychiatrists

Scene: the University of Cincinnati Medical School

Psychiatrists sit up straight in contoured chairs,
Not mentioning grace but opening brown bags
And looking inside to see what's going on.
They seem resigned to it. They take it out
And eat it with both hands. Some lick their fingers
Even cleaner. What little bits they drop
On the floor, they scuffle backwards casually
With their heels under their chairs and forget about.
They either talk with their mouths full or just chew
Dreamily into space, offering nothing
Out of their own bags and never asking
For something different from anybody else's.
Some crumple their bags, and some refold them empty
Along the original creases. And some unfold them
Again and check inside where the cake was.
They all applaud at the end after I've told them
Almost nothing about my mother and father,
Then turn aside and interrupt each other.

A Report on the Excavation

It seemed a promising dig: the slightly sunken
    Unnaturally level look of a campsite
        Repossessed by nature, by centuries
Of rain and wind. Our cross-trenching revealed,
    After the crusted dirt, a surprising stratum
        Of argilaceous shale (we had supposed
A more recent occupation), then limestone rubbish
    (A further surprise), but then at last
        (After this flood-borne silt and interbedding)
Another stratum of indurated soil
    Where pollen analysis indicated the presence
        Of wildflowers almost equally intermingled
With native weeds. From the regularity
    Of the outline, from the petrified remains
        Of a tree and an oblong structure
Resembling a gate (which was equally petrified)
    We have deduced a garden, though we have found
        Under the tumuli of apparent graves
No traces of humankind or of serpents, both
    Notoriously prone to scattering and dissolving
        Like feathers into innocent-seeming earth.

An Entomologist's Memo to Death

Dreamers have helped you fancy yourself a vampire.
They've given you black wings and a red smile
And called you out of the night to hide and seek
As they float in a drowse, their eyelids fluttering
Under your power in a dance for the living dead.

But reconsider that bat you impersonate.
Your paradigm has been sleeping upside down
All day and comes swooping, zigzagging, ravenous
For the savor of sweeter blood than human throats
Can offer the likes of you: the essence of moth.

At the first hint of your incisive squeaking
(Which a moth deciphers ten times farther off
Than you can detect the echo of its flight)
The moth has learned through sensors on its shoulders
Three subspecies of news to turn against you:

It knows how far you are by how clear you are;
Which way you are by which of its ears hears more
Of your needle-pointed song; your altitude
By your uninterrupted note or your stuttering
Between the interference of its wing beats.

And it swivels to fly straight the other way
Instantly, Death, exactly the wrong direction
For you to puzzle it out by what comes back
From its most narrow and most echoless profile.
If all goes well, you don't know what you've missed.

What happens next is nothing like the tales
You like to spin about that appetite
You snicker over and act so suave about
At dawn as you hang by your toes or hide in a box:
Your mouth is stuffy as moths, but most get away.

Epithalamion

They're getting married outdoors, and the wedding party,
    After much haphazard parking
        Along a narrow road, is making its way
Slowly under a canopy of cedars
    Beside a pool and slowly along a creek
        In the city arboretum. The bride and groom
Are in white. Her frothy veil
    Is pouring down from a clutch of baby's breath,
        An upright sprig of which
Is pinned to his lapel. They're struggling to lead
    An uneven line of bridesmaids and better men
        Who are lifting their white shoes
Straight up, then almost straight down again
    Into the muddy turf, their elbows out
        For balance. A slower, heavier procession
Of cold sober relatives and their offspring
    And friends and grim parents
        Is bringing up the rear, some cradling
Armloads of cut flowers. This must have seemed
    A wonderful idea months ago,
        Maybe in memory of their love and/or
Love-making in the semi-natural world,
    But today they find themselves gathered together
        In the sight of a pastor wearing an overcoat
Against the spring chill. He's standing in a gazebo,
    Fidgeting and looking slightly annoyed
        At all the scuffing and stomping. The loving couple
Has composed its own original
    Order of service. She holds a piece of paper.
        He holds a piece of paper. The pastor unfolds

His piece like an unsuccessful origami,
  And then they all take turns
    Asking and answering while cameras
Flash, and the couple kisses, and others kiss
  And embrace and pose and smile and shake hands
    And straggle back toward their cars,
Some taking time to frown uncertainly
  At the man with a notebook, sitting beside the pool,
    Who lifts his open hand at them
Ambiguously, meaning maybe *Bless you*
  Or *Fear not* or *I have several questions*
    Concerning you and these dragonflies
Darting and hovering in mating pairs
  Over the beautifully disordered, already fallen
    Petals of apple blossoms.

Eating a Toad

Each morning when we wake, said Emile Zola,
   We must eat our daily toad. We have to face being
      Merely ourselves again, not less revolting
Dream selves. But consider those toads who have gone
   Far, far out of their ways to be disgusting,
      To warn all predators they're not simply
Inedible, but can make a poisonous mouthful,
   Which as a first line of defense is as good as most
      Last lines. Almost nothing on earth
Will willingly and knowingly eat a toad
   Except a hedgehog, a creature
      Of modest habits and even more
Modest intentions. It moves slowly
   In a semi-private world it must surely wish
      Were even more private. Because it can outrun
So few others among the living, it settles
   For legless or torpid insects, dozing snakes,
      Or birds' eggs it can always depend on
To hold still. It can't see far enough
   Ahead or behind to avoid the foxes and badgers
      And dogs that would eat it in spite
Of its rough spines and its inconvenient tactic
   Of curling its body into a tight
      Unmanageable ball
And playing dead, and so, long before now,
   It would have been more scarce than the likes
      (And the admirably articulated dislikes)
Of Emile Zola if it hadn't had the foresight
   To overtake occasionally a complacent
      Toad, chew down that nearly lethal morsel,

And be heartily sick of it, foam at the mouth,
  Then carefully lick itself all over
    With the results: the awful armor of Toadhood.

4

In a Storm

They climbed the steep ridge slowly, saving each breath
　　For breathing, their boots unsure
　　　　Of the way without a path. Their only guide
Was steepness. Beyond the last trees, in a clearing,
　　A different, colorless light
　　　　Was falling. When they stepped into it,
They came to a sheer drop-off. They sank
　　To their knees and then lay trembling
　　　　On stone, felt suddenly as cold
As the stone was. They were above
　　The wind-tossed crowns of cedars. They were staring
　　　　Down at too much empty air. Beside them,
Trees were growing from rock, their gnarled
　　Weather-shaped limbs turned bare and bony
　　　　To windward, and stumps as gray as driftwood
Hung from fractured ledges. Their fingers touched
　　Fan lichen and blueberry, naming them,
　　　　Cliff-brake, penstemon, and moonwort,
As if saying, *These are alive like us,*
　　And they live here. Over the woods below,
　　　　A sweep of clouds came rolling toward them,
Rising along the cliff-side, churning
　　And flinging streamers of rain
　　　　Upward against their faces. A swirl of sleet
Swept past them, lashing, flew straight up
　　And was gone into white air
　　　　Above them, whirled, and came down
As a squall of hail like the ghosts of salmon eggs,
　　And simultaneous thunder and lightning
　　　　Struck, shaking the ridge. They held

To stone. They held still. They held themselves
And then each other. They had forgotten
Everything they had known except each other.

An Invitation at the Edge of a Desert

On the one side, a few bushes, and on the other,
    Sand and sandstone clear to the skyline.
        The last tree must have been somewhere
Back of beyond. The next is so far over
    And under the horizon, it may not even
        Be there. Can either of us remember
Why we were going to walk on sand
    Instead of turning around and heading back
        To wherever that was
We thought we were? While we wait here for an answer,
    Partner, let's dance. I don't know
        Of anyone but you worth dancing with
Or for or around or about and no other music
    Like this sighing of the wind just barely
        Underlying our breath. There's almost nothing
For us to kill underfoot at the outer edge
    Of human nurturing. From here on,
        It's all inhuman. Isn't it up to us
To look as foolish or as lightly fantastic
    As tricks of the desert air? The setting sun
        Is making us both seem brilliant
At least on one side. On the other, it gives us,
    Longer than any natural light
        Behind us, inseparable shadows.

Moon Dance

After her pummeling, after those trillions
   Of bombardments of heavenly hellfire
      And brimstone, the scourings and upheavals,
The showers of wild ashes
   And dust and the slashing streaks
      And pockmarks, we're here to tell this night
She's glistered them all over and is pouring
   Her riches, her pale treasure into our hands
      And across the crescents of our faces
Against what would have been darkness but for her,
   And even the blown roses beside us,
      Now the least likely to succeed in the garden,
Are still being transformed
   Into their younger selves and are quivering
      Under her touch and wavering closer,
And our lighter halves (no matter where we turn
   Or how we change or move) are gliding smoothly
      Over their own shadows, covered with moonlight.

In the Fog

That evening, they walked in fog, trying to be
    Romantic about it, though not over-fond
        Of their own confusion. They could see almost
Ten yards ahead and around them
    And, overhead, the near equivalent
        Of the zero underfoot. They thought they knew
Where they were as well as they knew each other.
    They recognized the street, the concrete sidewalk,
        Even their neighbor's trees like the palms of their hands.
They could have bet their lives they were something less
    Than fifty yards from home. Their memories
        Assured them it was there, beyond that vapor
Rolling in from the sea and interfering
    With the remains of sundown. If they had kept
        Standing there, if they hadn't moved
Forward then, they'd never have known
    What they know now. They took one hesitant step
        Together and another and quickly two more
And two more and even began
    Strolling along toward the virtual semblance
        Of what they thought was theirs. They wanted to see
So they could believe again. But daylight
    Or dark, in every weather since, stark sunlight
        Or moonless midnight, that whiteness follows them.

Trying to Help a Stranger

She was standing on the curb by the open door
    Of her car on the steep street while traffic
        Went grudging by, clogged, the other drivers
Resenting the blocked lane, and I was walking
    Toward her along the sidewalk. She held herself
        Stiffly to keep from falling, her body
Already almost falling as if to sleep
    Inside her dress, her face turning aside,
        Neither young nor old but gray as a blind spot.
When I started toward the driver's seat, she said *No*
    And held my sleeve. I tried to tell her
        I wasn't a thief. I put my arm around her
And said I was afraid she was in danger.
    She could be run over. I said I wanted to help her
        Drive somewhere safe. If she abandoned her car
It would be hauled away. She dropped her shoulder
    Out from under my arm like a dancing partner
        Hearing the first strains of the wrong music,
And said *No* again and again. Our eyes
    Had not met once. I touched her cold fingers,
        And in the dream I left her standing there.

Sleeping Alone

It should be easy, no one
    Else breathing beside you
And no restless turning
    Away and, look,
No hands or uneven feet
    In the wrong nightmare
And no murmuring heart
    Open or shut now, sighing
For you or yours but yours
    Alone this night, oblivion
Not yours for the asking
    Or begging, but the surprising
Glimmer of dawn, even there
    In that place somewhere
The other has gone to sleep
    Without you, not now
And then, but forever.

5

Partners in Crime:
A Sequence

Wanted

By the stamp machine, they hang on their own hooks,
Looking our way and sideways—the butterfly men
And women, black-and-white forgers and check-kiters,
The ones whose fingers disappeared in desk drawers

Among petty cash, whose credit cards, like their hearts,
Belonged to somebody else, the paperhangers
Who came up short, the boosters whose overcoats
Had more room on the inside than the outside.

Somebody wants them now. They always knew
Somebody wanted them and was holding out
Eager arms for them and wanted to keep them
Close for years and treat them as seriously

As people and were trying to find them
And give them a place to stay and help them learn
What was so hard to remember—the difference
Between two wrongs and a right. But they're all off

Far away somewhere, trying out new routines
And numbers and signatures and still hoping
Up against our wall they'll be forgiven
And forgotten even sooner than possible.

The Lookout

Your job is to wait outside and be nobody
   Standing there alone, spending some time,
     Not moving, not even making much
Of a shadow. You have to think
   Like someone who doesn't care
     What's going on around this fucking place
Which is so familiar, you don't notice it
   Or anything else really. You have to look
     As if you're waiting for nothing
To happen here, as usual. After all
   It's your neighborhood, and you're not expecting
     Something new out of line. You're only
Here again. If somebody walking by
   Looks your way, wondering maybe
     What you've got in mind or figuring
Shouldn't they know you from sometime or somewhere,
   You have to seem like you're only doing that door
     A favor by leaning on it. You don't fidget
Or fool around. You keep your hands
   Out of sight, minding their own business
     And empty. You're only killing
Time while your eyes and ears are listening
   And looking out for the first flashes, the wailing,
     Wailing in the distance, both coming closer,
And then you earn your share of whatever
   This is, whatever this turns out to be
     By beating your fist on the door and disappearing.

The Kidnapper

Sometime after midnight she'd been taken
   Out of her bed, out of her own room,
      And out of her house and carried somewhere
By a strange man in the dark to another house
   And another room and put in a different bed
      Blindfolded and left there
Alone till morning. Then he allowed her
   A little to eat and drink, but the questions
      She tried to ask him, one word
At a time with her tongue and both her lips
   And with all her heart, he didn't answer. She tried
      To tell him. She told him and told him
To listen to her before it was too late
   To save them both, to believe
      He mustn't harm her, must let her go
Back to her own room while they pretended
   Nothing had happened. She was appealing
      To his better nature. Wouldn't he rather
Look into her eyes by daylight now
   With his own eyes, face to face? No matter what
      Ransom he might ask, there was no one
Willing or able to pay, only herself
   Who had nothing to give
      But herself, and she listened behind the gauze
And waited and heard nothing but someone breathing
   Deliberately, quietly, painfully,
      Just out of reach.

The Detective

When he arrives, the worst has already happened,
    And half of what went wrong
        Has become the remains lying in front of him,
Unable to move. It consists of clothing,
    Terminal carbohydrates, and pieces of paper
        Now to be reorganized
As Before and After. The other half is gone,
    Having slipped away, perhaps who knows
        In disguise, and here at the scene of the crime
The search begins. Around him, a locked room
    Where something doesn't seem right, where everything
        Freezes: cold objects in the forms
Of people. He watches the corners
    Of their eyes and the places where their lips
        Seem edgy as shadows, all ending around
Other corners. Now he waits to hear
    Oddities, what doesn't fit, what doesn't quite
        Make sense: the man had noticed something
Unusual, but wasn't sure. The woman had thought
    Something very strange
        Had to be happening. The close friend
Hadn't been herself. The beautiful neighbor
    Felt she had lost touch. He invites them all
        To an innocent evening. He shows the stains,
The unaccountable indentations in cushions,
    The dregs in the sweating glass, the trembling
        Fingerprints here and here, and there
The suspicious persons who never dream
    They're reenacting the crime with their front views
        And profiles registered on every side

Of their faces as they tell stories. When it breaks,
    It breaks quickly, suddenly opens up
        And comes clean. It doubles over
Weeping and weaving in and out
    Of character, holding nothing back and holding
        Its head like a blunt instrument nobody
Wants to blame or confess to, and the detective
    Takes it into custody, leads it away
        And leaves no traces but some matters of fact.

The Getaway

They had to act natural. They had to look like
   They were still parts of an ordinary day
      Together on the sidewalk across the street
To the unfamiliar car, yet they had to be
   Quick about it without running. They had to think
   Like themselves but look like other people
Taking those steps, remembering, knowing
   Every foot they could put between their bodies
   And the scene behind them, where the noise
Of buzzers and bells and yowling
   And terribly shocked voices was growing
   Louder and louder. They pulled away
As calmly as possible, staring straight ahead
   Straight-faced, not glancing once
   To either side or backward, let alone
At each other, and took a turn in the most unlikely
   Direction they could think of. Under the limit,
   They drove steadily, legally toward home.

6

The Fire-bringers

You see it first as a spark on the horizon
Like a distant campfire, but instead of dwindling
As daylight dwindles, slowly it comes closer.
You see the fire-bringer now, the exhausted runner
You've waited for, legs almost giving in
As he stumbles forward, staring, his mouth gaping
Like an old young man at the end of a nightmare.

And you reach out for the torch before it falls
From his numb fingers, take it and turn away
To start across long stretches of broken ground
In the pitch of the night, your shadow (an outcast
Whose feet slip swiftly and surely underfoot
At every stride) bearing you up, but holding
Nothing against the earth, while you hold light.

But soon each breath goes, shallower, emptier,
No matter how deep you draw it. Each breath
Is casting its own shadow through your body,
Taking your breath away as if you'd caught it
Only to find it gone, to be caught again
And lost again, till its pathway burns more fiercely
than yours or the flame's, now growing heavier

In your clenched fist. Your shadow joins the dance
Of two lame feet in time to your blood's drumming,
And there ahead, half light, half shade, another
Fire-bringer waits for you, one hand reaching out
Toward yours as you lunge to clasp it, to hang on
For dearer and dearer life. He takes your fire
And runs away with it into darkness.

Sentry

Attention. You'll begin right here on the dot
 Of midnight and, till dawn, you'll wear
  A path between this place and that other place
Over there. Then you'll pause and about-face
 And come back here and do likewise, always
  On the alert, your ears and your rifle cocked
For something not in the book. You're looking out
 For suspicious forms. You see one, you say,
  Halt! Who goes there? And tonight's password
Is silence. Nothing at all, since no one
 Is supposed to be up or even out and about
  But you and the enemy. You do your part
At the outer line of defense. Your purpose is
 To keep those people lying there behind you
  Safe in their beds. Most of them have fallen
Through the door of Dreamland now, and they're depending
 On you and others like you to let them go
  On and on drowsing and slumbering and snoring
Without coarse nightmares about anything
 Too ugly creeping up over the edge
  Of their mattresses across their sheets to the craters
Of their pillow slips and into the privacy
 Of their semicircular canals. Your aim
  Is to stay awake at all costs. Of course you may
Relax once in a while, sit down and take your time
 To mull things over. The most creative forces
  Don't use up all their energy pacing back
And forth, and isn't the goal of all our conflicts
 The achievement of equilibrium? Just think
  Of peace and quiet. The voice of the enemy

Can be profoundly restful. Why not end
    All these hostilities by laying down
        The law for the soothing Pax Romana of sleep?

The Secret Agent

He remembered clearly his instructor's voice
    Telling him how to work at being a man
        In a safe house on a street in a neighborhood
With access to a city which needed to be
    Understood and disarmed. He was to think
        Of himself, not as an enemy
Among enemies, but as a citizen
    Of a nation founded on two rooms and a bath
        And a lock without a foreign policy
Or an intelligence. He was to remain
    Unobtrusively anonymous,
        To take no offense at the behavior of strangers
With stranger customs than he'd been trained to enjoy
    Or mimic. He was to be at one
        Remove, to save his identity
For his bad dreams, to keep his promises
    Strictly to himself and become a mailbox
        For carefully sealed encrypted messages
Describing what might change this side of the world
    To the other side and bring to an end
        The separation of powers. Unfortunately,
Though he wrote with invisible ink and listened
    Through walls and wires and concrete and thin air
        To another silence and disguised his voice
Even when alone, he gave himself away,
    Betrayed himself with careless slips of the tongue,
        With tics and gestures memorized in a lifetime
Unconsciously out of control in the wrong country,
    And like even the most scrupulous imposters
        On earth, he found those habits impossible

To alter or avoid or do without
   In his unguarded moments. So now he must learn
     To do without all his unguarded moments.

Floating

"Thousands of American servicemen in World War II
drowned in water less than ten feet deep during Pacific
invasions because they didn't know how to swim or float."
—*Red Cross Swimming Instructor's Manual*

Your landing craft, dead in the water, has landed
    Hard on a reef and is sinking
A mile from shore, and you can see an island
    Farther away and smaller
Than any postcard from home. You're overboard
    And you're going to be under
Your own command now, or else
    Be lost at sea, so your first order
Is to give up and forget
    Your rifle, your ammunition, your empty helmet,
Your boots, and everything else
    You were never attached to, and to surrender
To water and lie back, disarmed, with both your arms
    And your eyes wide open under a sky
Also wide open, no longer to be thought of
    As a container of aircraft or bursting clouds
Or streaks of shellfire
    But as a source of comfort, a reminder
Of the right direction to be breathing
    In and out. You must understand
Everything around you is heavier and therefore
    Less buoyant than you are. You have to trust
Your body to rise to this occasion
    Like the jellyfish Man-of-War. And there
You are, and what will become of you
    Is in your hands in one of the many forms
Of the ocean which you can hold for a moment
    And again after a moment at arm's length

And put behind you. You should aim for the shore
    However loud or obscured by smoke it may seem,
However dangerous, even lethal
    It is compared to what's become of you:
A clearer, simpler version of what you thought
    You were, the bare essentials of a man
Looking for something
    Solid to touch, not even necessarily
A place to stand, but to know again
    On all fours as somewhere to lie down.

What to Do When Surrounded

In a tactical sense, you have become nothing
    But flanks. To such fundamental questions
        As *Where Is the Enemy?* and *Where*
Should I Direct My Fire? your answers
    Have been reduced to a simple minimum:
        Anywhere and Everywhere. Only one
Question will have a recreational value:
    Where Is the Enemy's Weakness? You may dig in
        And hope incompetent or lunatic
Enfilading fire, brought on by hubris,
    Will cause your enemy to decimate
        His opposite numbers firing the opposite way.
Meanwhile, you may stand indifferently
    And casually upright in the midst of battle
        Through shot and shell, facing at every turn
A circular firing squad, may brandish the banner
    With the strange device of your country
        Right or wrong at the heart
Of this debacle, unless those colors seem
    In the end less subtle
        Than the shades of your uniform
And your skin, which were intended
    To blend with the earth, to form a useful part
        Of your more natural surroundings.

In Rubble

Right after the bomb, even before the ceiling
   And walls and floor are rearranging
      You and themselves into a different world,
You must hold still, must wait for them
   To settle down in unpredictable ways,
      To bring their wars, shuddering,
To an end, and only then should you begin
   Numbly to feel what freedom may be left
      To your feet or knees, to your elbows
Or clenched fingers. Where you used to walk
   Or lean or lie down or fix your attention
      At a whim or stomp your foot
Or slump in a chair, you'll find a new
   Architecturally unsound floor-plan
      To contend with, if you can move
At all. Now you may remember others
   Who were somewhere near you before
      This breakdown of circumstances. Caught by surprise
Like you, they may be waiting separately
   At their own levels, inside their own portions
      Of your incoherent flat. They may be thinking
Of you, as you are of them, and wondering
   Whether some common passageway, no matter
      How crooked or narrow, might still exist
Between you, through which you might share the absence
   Of food and water and the cold comfort
      Of daylight. They may be expecting you
To arrive at any moment, to crawl through dust
   And fire to their rescue as they find their bodies
      Growing more stiff, assuming even more

Unusual attitudes at every turn
  Of a second hand, at every sound
    Of a bell or an alarm, at every pounding
Of a door or a heart, so if you can't reach them
  Now and they can't reach you, remember, please
    Remember, whatever you say,
Whatever you hear or keep to yourself, whatever
  You scream or whisper, will need to make
    Some kind of sense, perhaps for days and days.

Sleeping in a Ditch

You'll be by the side of a road. You'll be too far
    From where you were going—somewhere
        Under a roof—and you won't have any place
To turn except to the ditch beside you, nowhere
    Out of sight of people who wouldn't be happy
        To see you out in the open
At the wrong time where you have no business
    Being, somebody else's property
        Where you need to have the right clothes
And the right kind of name and numbers
    On pieces of paper in your pockets. A ditch
        Is safer than it looks. Though you have no fire
And no ceiling, your walls go on and on
    And are bulletproof, and if something wants to hurt you
        From overhead, it has to have good aim
Like rain or snow. And nothing will notice you
    From far away. You no longer look like someone
        Who doesn't belong, standing on a horizon,
A silhouette, an easy target. Now you look like
    Where you are. You can almost remember
        Fighting for something. You stood up
For your convictions, but now you're crouching
    And lying down for them. Wildflowers
        And weeds and escaped roses have come here
Seasons ago and have stayed, and rainwater
    Has fallen and gone to earth and gathered
        And stayed again. If you had time,
You could make yourself at home
    Among these others who've come and gone
        To sleep, who've bedded themselves down

Without anyone's permission but their own
This evening which is already turning slowly
All by itself like you into nighttime.

7

A Woman Driving a Car Full of Flowers

Side by side, we've stopped for the same light,
And I have just enough time to recognize
The dahlias in clumps, the roses of every shade
And patent intermingled with aliens

And nosegays of pansies with their faces pressed
To the inside of the windows like snotty kids
In a school bus. Beside her, an upright stand
Of quivering gladioli is riding shotgun.

Is she the mother of mothers on her way
To an April shower? A one-car funeral?
A nurse ripping off a whole floor of a hospice?
Some stalks are bending halfway over her shoulder

Like back-seat drivers, but she doesn't appear
To mind them. She's dressed to kill. She's suited and coifed
And hatted and possessed. She cases herself
In the rear-view mirror, dabbles with lipstick,

Mumbles it, then beams at the fresh results
And turns them toward me. Now catching the green,
She leads us forward into the afternoon
And evening to the end of a rootless garden.

Have You Any Questions about Your Garden?

The gardener on TV wants me to think
About fertilizer. He wants me to take advantage
Of him and the season, which are apparently
Almost free of charge at the end of winter.

He'd like me to get busy and prepare
My plots, planters, beds, borders, and pots
With his blades, clippers, trowels, and pitchforks,
His rakes, hoes, hoses, and wheels within wheels.

He has, in both his clutches, packets of seeds
Like embryonic beanstalks or rainbows
Or dark-of-the-moon dust, and he's offering me
All of them for my own while there's still time

To put them where they'll prosper. Oh, he wants me
To take them off his hands or they'll go to someone
Who loves his or her garden more than I do
And understands what's beautiful and good

For him or her. He'll even throw in bulbs
If I hurry, and he wants me to quit listening
And get on the phone and put something in order
Around my colorless house before it's too late

To do anything except with a weed-whacker.

At the Edge of a Clear-cut Forest

"A town is saved, not by any righteous men in it, but by the
woods and swamps that surround it."
—Thoreau, *Journal,* July, 1850

The righteous men were here to level the trees
And take them away. They've filled the nearby swamp.
They've gone to enlighten the eyes and sharpen the ears
Of creatures in another part of the forest.

I can see both sides of the divide from here.
Numberless platforms for the deliverance
Of stump speeches, though the audience
In the woods has drawn back carefully into hiding

Or slid among the cattails and shallow pools
Where the creek was. I'm here to repeat myself
In a declaration the trees make without words.
They repeat themselves in spite of righteous men.

My fellow citizens, come, come and be saved
By a better town than yours. What's left of it
Has better schools and nurseries and far more
Honest, forgiving police, waste management,

Recycling, civic choirs and soloists,
Home care for the dying, immediate reemployment
Of the dead, and panic in its most durable form:
The power, the living end of astonishment.

A Falling Tree

If a tree falls in the woods and no one
is there to hear it, does it make any sound?
—an old problem for philosophy students

The professor posed the question, and we sat there
    Like thousands of dutiful and sleepy others
        Before us, trying more or less to remember
How we might separate impulse from response
    And stimulus from the source
        Of stimulus, and we had the discussion
And the polite arguments he was hoping to hear,
    But all that day through other disciplines
        And in my room that night, the tree
Kept falling in my mind, and went on
    Falling now and then, and was still falling
        When my more philosophical classmates
Had moved ahead with a slow deliberate
    Thoughtful reluctance into the minefields
        Of the Theological Problem, and it fell
So often for me, I began to wonder: if no one
    Is in those woods, how can I keep seeing
        The tree falling? If I can imagine it,
Isn't that noise in my imagination
    As real as a falling tree? I could close my eyes
        And see it and hear it
Crackle and whisk and shudder as it toppled
    And swept along the trunks of some still standing
        And screamed before the boom
And the death rattle and sigh
    And the reverberant silence, the same silence
        It would make from then on, as it hollowed itself

And rotted for the sake of generations
   To come, which would rise and fall whether or not
      Anyone wanted to be there, listening.

Burnt Offering

Suddenly he was caught
   In a thicket, his horns
      Were caught, the curving, hard
Pride of his head was tangled
   Among thorns and brambles,
      And his thickly curled coat
Snagged as if by teeth, his neck
   Held even more tightly
      Than by a shepherd's crook
And made to hold still. He had been grazing
   In a field with quiet ewes,
      With spring lambs leaping
As if dancing from stone to stone
   On a mountainside. Now he struggled
      To think of what had trapped him
Here, what lamb-like mistake
   He'd made, but only remembered
      A voice commanding him
(More loudly, more fiercely, more terribly,
   Than any dog). Through bushes he saw
      A boy bringing dead branches,
Dragging them to a heap and kneeling
   And lighting them with sparks
      Struck from between stones,
And an old man (bent over his own
   Grizzled bellwether's beard)
      Coming toward him, holding a knife
And smiling, both of them smiling
   As if already sitting down together
      To warm themselves by a fire.

The Son of a Carpenter

He knew the shapes and the gnarled persuasions
   Of wood, how it could be made
      To hold itself together, even in pieces,
With or against its grain, upright
   Or level or at some human angle
      With mortise and tenon, with dovetails,
And how, seasoned and cured and stained,
   It could be depended on to serve
      More than one lifetime, though it might lose
Its firmness if allowed to suffer too long
   In water or fire. He knew how it could rot,
      Be warped or broken, but revered it
For what it might become. He had seen it turn
   Under his hands from its raw nature
      To something longer lasting and man-made,
Made beautiful by chisel and adze and plane,
   By surrender under the iron teeth
      Of the saw and the slamming down
Of the hammer, again and again
   Driving the nails home. He knew enough
      To rest at the end of days against a tree,
In its brief shade, leaning back
   Awkwardly but gratefully
      Against the living wood that had taken
Its own shape before his and could make him
   Give in to it. He would have time
      To wonder then (as his eyes wandered
Down across empty fields to the beginning
   Of the desert) why the groves of his occupation
      And his father's were falling, even as he kept watch.

Big Game

You're feeling pleased with yourself, perhaps even
    Beside yourself as you approach slowly
The big game animal you've shot
    And think is dead. It doesn't move. It's no longer
Far away, out of reach, something painfully
    Beautiful and dangerous that wasn't yours
But seemed what you'd always wanted
    To be close to. Now you have it, have it right here
Holding still for you. Listen now. Listen.
    Look carefully: if its eyes are wide open
Like yours, if they're fixed and glassy, if the flies
    Have already come to call, then you're home
More or less free and you've done more
    Or less what you thought you'd aimed to do
When you came here with a gun,
    And this no longer animated body
Is all yours now, a prize to be taken away
    And eaten or otherwise disposed of, to be mounted
And preserved for the benefit of other eyes
    And ears for the rest of your hunting life. But
        remember
As you bend near this creature, smiling,
    Already rehearsing the modest parts you'll play
At your comfortable fireside in the glow
    Of before-and-after-dinner stories, look out
For yourself (it may already be too late,
    But look out anyway) because if its eyelids
Are shut, if you can't see the light
    Between them, it's still alive. It may be trying

Hard to remain itself, a skill much harder
    To learn than you might imagine, and if your hand
Should touch what's left of it anywhere at all,
    It may suddenly show you something you've neglected
To learn in time: the surprisingly quick, inhuman,
    Deadly, unmanly art of self defense.

That Hunter

That Bella Coola hunter had followed and found
   Every kind of creature in the mountains,
      In the woods, and along rivers
And had killed them, had praised them
   Over their still warm bodies, and thanked them
      For dying, for becoming carcasses
He carried back to the fire-pit
   Where he would sit and eat them and listen
      As his wife and children thanked him
By mumbling and humming
   To themselves and swallowing and becoming
      Part of what was his. He would tell them
(Through a mask of firelight) how he had seen
   And known the breath of Mountain Goat
      White on the mountainside, how the breath
Of Black Bear had been black at the cave's mouth,
   How the breath of Grizzly Bear against the sky
      Had been a rainbow, and he smiled
Inside himself without moving his lips
   And ate the most tender flesh of the inner thighs
      Of Snow-That-Does-Not-Fall, the strong, melting
Tongue of Crooked Foot, and even the many-colored
   Brittle splinters behind the eyes of He-Is-
      Coming-Toward-You, and he became
A great hunter, and one morning he hunted
   Along the ice and through the forest
      And along the riverbank to the end where its mouth
Opened and saw nothing but the blood-colored smoke
   Of Bax-bakwa-lanux-siwe—He-Eats-
      What-Cannot-Be-Eaten—and tracked him down

And killed him and ate his heart, but suddenly saw him
    Leap away and around on all four winds
        As sand-fleas, clouds of mosquitoes, and horseflies.

Madman

When the Haida heard him and found him in the woods
  Shouting at trees and bushes
    As if they were enemies and saw him scowling
At the sky and his own body and saying out loud
  The forbidden names of the dead and saw him turning
    And dancing on stiff legs and opening
And shutting his mouth, biting the air
  And eating it, they gathered around him
    And held him, shook him, and shook their heads
And told him they were sorry. They rubbed his shoulders
  And smoothed his hands and arms
    And his quivering back while the Dreamer
Went to the river and brought uprooted strands
  Of white-water crowfoot and tied them
    Around his neck. They left him there
Still staring and dancing, still shouting
  At everything he could name around him
    Or at what he couldn't name or at nothing
After the moon rose. But beginning
  Deep in the night, the crowfoot hanging
    Against his breath, against his heart,
Held him still, quieted him, and told him
  To sleep now and to wait till morning,
    Then go with it to the river to remember
Their roots in water, themselves floating,
  Themselves knowing their pathways, themselves
    Quick, themselves again in the light.

For a Newborn Muskrat

It has risen now, just now, to the surface
    Of the muddy water and keeps itself
        Afloat, just barely, by an already floating
Stem of a marsh bellflower, the pale claws
    Of one nearly hairless forefoot wavering there,
        Above the flooded den where its mother
Is going to think of something else. It stretches
    Forward with another half-webbed foot
        And draws it back again into a dream
Of swimming, of imagining no longer
    Holding on to the stem, its half-shut eyes
        Dark between pink lids as it takes in
One breath, and another after
    Another, takes in the cloudy light of the ditch
        By the logging road and the cold light of the world.

Snakeskin

All day those eyes
Staring from burnt-gold
Irises at nothing, glazed
Over like pebbles etched
And blurred by sand
Above a mouth shut thin
Where the fangs lay folded,
And the wedge of the skull
Strained slowly forward,
Forward again against stone,
And then the skin gave way
Like a cloud parting,
And the other, dazzled
And glistening, entered
The world again head first,
Came forward into the sun,
Came forward to uncoil,
Turning its crown aside
Out of the light and was gone,
And the perfect sheath,
Each scale to the last
Pale link of the rattle still
What it had been, went tumbling
Slowly adrift downwind.

After the Eruption

After the many deaths down burning wind
And the downfall of forests, fire streams, vine lightning,
Rockfall, rose-madder dawns, after moons less gray
Than ashfall across what had been a mountain meadow
Now broken to ash-drift—suddenly, dead silence
For days, for seasons, for years, and now slowly
In rain, fireweed and lupine lifting leaves
Half open, half-inch by inch, straining
With bracken, horsetail, and pearly everlasting
To break the crust, all spreading into the light,
And willow and cottonwood by the choked streams
And alder where, under shade, the pines and firs
Beside the burial mounds of their ancestors
Begin again the climb toward a timberline.

Crossing the Divide

You stand at the top of a ridge and, stretched below you,
See a wild valley down to a wild river,
And if you, this night,
Are to lie by that riverside, you must make your way
As water would through gullies and spurred ravines
In a rite of passage.

One step, and each bush, each wildflower will be holy,
Each stone a dangerous god. From every pool
And spring where you kneel
The lips of a god will rise to meet your lips
And will drink from yours. Each turn of wind, each bird cry
Will quaver a warning.

You will carry a different name now without knowing
What it is. It will be there in your face,
In your empty hands,
In the way you walk or lie down, in how you breathe.
You will be known all day by what you do,
Not what you were.

You will walk among the scattered bones of the dead
Who came, like you, to see the gods throw aside
Feathers and rain,
The glitter of standing water, the masks of bedrock,
Moss and dead trees, to be by nightfall
Not dust but singing.

8

Self-portrait Ending with a Found Poem from
Life Histories of North American Birds

All morning, I had been brooding
   In a marsh, trying to go on
      Naming what I could believe in:
A toad being itself
   In the glowing yellow hood
      Of a skunk cabbage, in a thicket
A salamander whose light
   Of day was a shadow
      Cast by the false leaf
Of a quillwort, and the lovely
   Wreckage of cup fungus,
      And then I was standing
Still, still thinking
   Of what they were
      To me, all by themselves
Here, like me, nowhere
   But here, and then I saw
      What I had been
Seeing without seeing
   What it was, so near me,
      I might have touched him
After two more steps—
   A bittern hunched
      Among cattails, his beak upright
Like the snag of the stump
   He meant to be, as long
      As I was there. The only eye
I could see or see with
   Was open only halfway
      But like mine was staring

At mine and at his
    Without blinking, without
        The least misunderstanding
Of what we were or where
    Or why. *No doubt*
        He enjoys himself
After his own fashion,
    But his notions of happiness
        Are peculiar. He prefers
Solitude, and he leads
    The eccentric life
        Of a recluse, "forgetting
The world and by the world
    Forgot." To see him
        At his ordinary occupation,
One might fancy him shouldering
    The solution of some problem
        Of vital consequence. He waits
Motionless, his head drawn in,
    His eyes half closed as if
        In profound meditation,
Or he steps about
    In a devious way
        With an absent-minded air,
And for greater seclusion,
    He will even hide
        In a thick brush clump
For hours together,
    But if startled in his retreat
        While his thinking cap is on,
He will seem dazed, like one
    Suddenly aroused
        From a deep sleep. As soon
As he collects his wits
    And remembers unpleasantly
        That the outside world

Exists, he will be common-
 Sensical enough to beat
  A hasty retreat from altogether
Too much action for his nature,
  Which is what he did. He rose
   On wings the color of bark
From the shade, in the ascendant,
  His muddy, uprooted legs
   Trailing him out of sight.

In a Landfill

Our city fathers and mothers picked this place
To file and forget whatever they don't want
Or can't stand or have no other idea
What to do with. They have it all hauled here
To be mashed and leveled and seeded by the wind
And left to percolate and brew
And settle to what they hope looks natural.

Because I feel obliged to contribute something
And not just stand here, I sit down. And at once
The old horizon is raked over
By bluegrass and tassels of wild oats and the crowned heads
Of Queen Anne's lace and other tough survivors
And aimless pioneers. Biologists say
You're seldom more than six feet from an ant,

And here they come to analyze my shoes
And the rest of me, which is more than I can do.
The ants and weeds and I have much in common:
We can cast shadows. We can metabolize
For a while. We can reflect daylight just as long
As it lasts. We can persist in the folly of being
Ourselves. We can add and multiply and divide.

We can disobey the laws of vagrancy,
Assembly, and trespass. We can feel inclined
To put our six-or-less, more-or-less best feet
Forward, backward, or deeper into the earth
Briefly before we lie down on our jobs,
Before we decide to lower our expectations
And join the rest, making ourselves scarce.

Standing Above the Fault Scarp

It's under you. You're moving, yet so slowly
   You only know you're going gradually
      Downhill by how the older trees all lean
One way above the grass, how standing here
   By a crooked house, you know yourself and the earth
      Lean that way too with the dragging (far down)
Of bedrock, far underneath a spillway
   Of deeper stones out of sight, out of mind,
      All waiting there for you like a riverbed.

Turning Over an Old Leaf

It's lying flat as if pressed as a keepsake
    By the night and the rain, a decoration
        For autumn on the opaque window
Of the sidewalk. When I half lift one edge,
    The infant earwigs and third-of-an-inch
        Millipedes go running away across
And under lopsidedly anywhere out
    Of sight in full-stress mode from a new
        Multidimensional world. Einstein told
The encyclopedia people there was no
    Agreed-upon definition of a surface
        To begin or end with. These agreeable creatures
Want to be somewhere under instead of over,
    Not vagabonding on a Mobius strip
        As parties to the uncontrollable
Manipulations of a god, but laboring
    Once more at their love on the other side of the sun
        And moon in an underworld, which now,
Even now, is rolling back to where it was
    In their good old days, where it belongs,
        More near, more edible than any heaven.

At the Mirror

You can take a good long look in there
    Now and again, like it or not,
        For practical reasons or to try
The over-ripe plums of self-regard
    One more time or to rub your nose in it,
        But that hand reaching toward you, ready
To shake all by itself on a bad bargain,
    Will stop short
        In spite of you, and those lips,
Whether pursed or sealed or loosely
    Disagreeable, no matter how
        Closely pressed or half open
To suggestion, will be smack
    Up against it. Your shifting, shifty,
        And shiftless eyes will tell you
Exactly what you deserve and may not want
    To know, and though you turn
        Till your peripheral vision blurs
At the bleary edge of your profile,
    You can be sure that Other is waiting to stare
        You down, or to finish the game and match
You eye to eye again, with an eye
    For an eye, till you flinch and slip away,
        Blinking, out of sight.

Instructions for Whistling in the Dark

Remember: you're demonstrating to Dark Powers
    That your lips aren't too dry to carry a tune
      As you pass what may well be the site
Of your near future. The key
    Is nonchalance. Your most dynamic range
      Is narrow: not the high squeal of a rabbit
Entertaining its first-last fox, no alarming
    Slurs or sloops. You want to give the impression
      The melody you make might just as well
Have been silence, as if whistling at all
    Were an afterthought or a casual exercise
      Of a skill too trivial to mention,
Like an ability to stroll now or to walk
    Slightly faster than that or even
      To jog or shift to the full length of a stride
More suitable for middle distances
    Or even the long run, reserving a clump
      In your gut for a final sprint, after which you'll be,
As like as not, under artificial light,
    Some bought-and-paid-for public illumination,
      Feeling relieved and ever so slightly
Foolish, winded, your lips pursed
    And still emitting now and then (almost
      Inaudibly) a vibrant column of air.

Trying to Fall Asleep Beside an Iguana

There on the fence beside me, he isn't thinking
    Of moving, his tail in sunlight,
        The rest of him in the shadow
Of a garden wall. His wide-open, white-gold eye
    Is telling me he knows far more
        Than I do about being awake
And asleep at the same time. I used to think
    I was born to offer skin and bones to the sun,
        Having basted them with potions like a wizard
Ready to fly away into the night
    Of his own daydreams. But this strange familiar
        Has already stared me down
From over the edge of my own darkness
    Twice, has made me blink
        And lose myself, then flinch
And startle awake to meet his eye
    Again as he cold-bloodedly outwaits
        Every change of my mind, still staring
From his superior post. He knows
    Which one of us will remain
        Truer to what he is, which one will be
More vivid in his place, be gray and green
    At once, whose withdrawn tongue
        Is more to the point, whose spine
Has crested in a ruffled and jaggedly spiked
    Sail in spite of this dead calm, whose throat
        Has blossomed in age and deepened, and which one
Knows better what to do about fruit flies
    Buzzing around ripe melon, and which of us
        Can be both here and out of sight in an instant.

Almost Waking Up in the Middle of the Night

You're not quite lying here. You seem aware
   Of a self half-melted, a liquified horizontal
      Impersonal mass suspended over a chasm
Filled with a darkness heavier than water,
   A different world where, till a breath ago,
      You'd been alive and well. It's still down there
But now you aren't. What are you going to do
   With this other life you're suddenly half-thinking
      Might be yours? You can tell this moment
Is after other moments, but none of them
   Are yours. You want to dissolve, to be reabsorbed
      By what lies under you. You want to vanish
Little by little into it, be disengaged
   In particles again through the colloidal
      Solution to all your problems. You remember
Come, Sleep, oh sweet deceiving, lull me
   In your delight a while and have the illusion
      You'd found down there the distillment
Of ease, a solemn stillness, a closing-down
   Of all your doors beyond which you'd become
      Nothing at all, and now you're falling out
Of this time and place into no time or place,
   And if you had a mouth and could still move it,
      You'd say you're going to be yourself again.

Good Night

You can't get excited about going to sleep.
—Roethke, *Straw for the Fire*

But you can, and if you do, expecting
   Altogether too much from one tomorrow,
      You can wrap your head in a good old-fashioned
Nightcap and be ear-plugged and eye-shaded
   And pillowed and nest-egged over and under down,
      Sheeted and blanketed and comforted
And made to feel as little
   As possible, so you'll hear nothing new or erroneus
      Like your own preambles and prefaces, the squeaks
And rumbles of the overture
   To that tone poem for basso and soprano,
      Uvula ostinato, and start flying
To the four unearthly corners of your eyes. Oh,
   Yes, you can get excited, but stark awake,
      No one will want to be near you when you go
Or when you arrive in a heap at the other side
   Of that bad night or hear you greeting the dawn
      With disappointment under the Xmas tree,
Tearing apart the glittering, breakable presents
   As savagely as the child you were or the bear
      You are, spreading himself at the picnic table.

The Old Man of the Woods

He was young, and he was hurrying into the forest
   As the sun went down, and all the demons
      Murmured in their sleep and woke
And sprang into branches and clung there,
   Pretending to be birds catching the last
      Of the vinegar-gold-green dying
End of daylight in their teeth
   As they snapped at his ears or, playing dead,
      Crouched behind bushes
And snickered at him, or squatted
   Like mossy stones and lay in wait
      Till he could blunder near enough
To be scratched. Or they clawed holes
   In the already humpbacked ground of the pathway
      To break his bones. He had nearly lost
His heart. His heart had almost forgotten
   How to beat and beat again. It couldn't tell him
      Why he'd run away from the cold hearth
In the empty house. Was he saving his poor mother?
   His poor father? His poor brother and sister?
      Or that terrified girl, her arms held out toward him
Over the shoulder of a shapeless stranger
   Running into the dark? In a dim clearing
      Where the sun had just this moment
Taken its light away, he stumbled
   To his knees and tried to remember how
      To breathe and saw an old man
Sitting among shadows, his face hidden, who said,
   "Lie down. The morning is more clever
      Than evening." So he lay down and slept,

And small creatures, wearing their own fur,
  With one tail each, walking on four feet,
    Came out, one at a time, and touched him lightly
To see if he belonged with them at the beginning
  Of night, and very carefully made sure
    His eyes were closed, then left him
Where he was and went back to dreaming
  Of being demons again. He woke at dawn,
    As calm and clever as he would ever be.

At the Foot of a Mountain

You're at the end of the trail an hour before dawn.
   You've brought the hardware
      Of suspense and enough rope
For this vertical landscape. You've plotted the way
   On maps and have tried to calm yourself
      Into starting what you know, almost for certain,
You won't be able to do. You could pretend
   Your imaginary partner
      Has been taken ill or is missing. You could feel
Some plausible complaint, an authentic cramp
   Or the onset of a recurrent fever
      Or go lame, then limp away with no more
Dishonor than you might be able to stand,
   Given enough time. But despite what's drifting
      Suddenly across your eyes like snow
In a slow wind, like broken light, you can see
   All your old guides beside you, looking at you
      With a relaxed amusement. They're waiting
For you to understand again, to remember
   Turning back and the smug safety of breathing—
      More terrible in the end
Than ice-fall—and you realize if you stay
   They'll climb without you. They watch you now
      Lift one foot and put it slightly ahead
Of the other. You can see them moving
   On all sides of you and beginning,
      As you join in, their uninterrupted chanting.

DAVID WAGONER is the author of seventeen books of poems and ten novels, and editor of *Straw for the Fire: From the Notebooks of Theodore Roethke, 1943–63* (1972). He has received an American Academy of Arts and Letters award, the Sherwood Anderson Award, the Fels Prize, the Ruth Lilly Poetry Prize, the Eunice Tjetjens Memorial and English-Speaking Union prizes from *Poetry,* and fellowships from the Ford Foundation, the Guggenheim Foundation, and the National Endowment for the Arts. A former Chancellor of the Academy of American Poets, he was the editor of *Poetry Northwest* from 1966 until its last issue in 2002.

Illinois Poetry Series

Laurence Lieberman, Editor

Healing Song for the Inner Ear
Michael S. Harper (1984)

The Passion of the Right-Angled Man
T. R. Hummer (1984)

Dear John, Dear Coltrane
Michael S. Harper (1985)

Poems from the Sangamon
John Knoepfle (1985)

In It
Stephen Berg (1986)

The Ghosts of Who We Were
Phyllis Thompson (1986)

Moon in a Mason Jar
Robert Wrigley (1986)

Lower-Class Heresy
T. R. Hummer (1987)

Poems: New and Selected
Frederick Morgan (1987)

Furnace Harbor: A Rhapsody of the
North Country
Philip D. Church (1988)

Bad Girl, with Hawk
Nance Van Winckel (1988)

Blue Tango
Michael Van Walleghen (1989)

Eden
Dennis Schmitz (1989)

Waiting for Poppa at the
Smithtown Diner
Peter Serchuk (1990)

Great Blue
Brendan Galvin (1990)

What My Father Believed
Robert Wrigley (1991)

Something Grazes Our Hair
S. J. Marks (1991)

Walking the Blind Dog
G. E. Murray (1992)

The Sawdust War
Jim Barnes (1992)

The God of Indeterminacy
Sandra McPherson (1993)

Off-Season at the Edge of the World
Debora Greger (1994)

Counting the Black Angels
Len Roberts (1994)

Oblivion
Stephen Berg (1995)

To Us, All Flowers Are Roses
Lorna Goodison (1995)

Honorable Amendments
Michael S. Harper (1995)

Points of Departure
Miller Williams (1995)

Dance Script with Electric Ballerina
Alice Fulton (reissue, 1996)

To the Bone: New and Selected Poems
Sydney Lea (1996)

Floating on Solitude
Dave Smith (3-volume reissue, 1996)

Bruised Paradise
Kevin Stein (1996)

Walt Whitman Bathing
David Wagoner (1996)

Rough Cut
Thomas Swiss (1997)

Paris
Jim Barnes (1997)

The Ways We Touch
Miller Williams (1997)

The Rooster Mask
Henry Hart (1998)

The Trouble-Making Finch
Len Roberts (1998)

Grazing
Ira Sadoff (1998)

Turn Thanks
Lorna Goodison (1999)

Traveling Light:
Collected and New Poems
David Wagoner (1999)

Some Jazz a While:
Collected Poems
Miller Williams (1999)

The Iron City
John Bensko (2000)

Songlines in Michaeltree:
New and Collected Poems
Michael S. Harper (2000)

Pursuit of a Wound
Sydney Lea (2000)

The Pebble: Old and New Poems
Mairi MacInnes (2000)

Chance Ransom
Kevin Stein (2000)

House of Poured-Out Waters
Jane Mead (2001)

The Silent Singer:
New and Selected Poems
Len Roberts (2001)

The Salt Hour
J. P. White (2001)

Guide to the Blue Tongue
Virgil Suárez (2002)

The House of Song
David Wagoner (2002)

X =
Stephen Berg (2002)

Arts of a Cold Sun
G. E. Murray (2003)

Barter
Ira Sadoff (2003)

The Hollow Log Lounge
R. T. Smith (2003)

In the Black Window:
New and Selected Poems
Michael Van Walleghen (2004)

A Deed to the Light
Jeanne Murray Walker (2004)

Controlling the Silver
Lorna Goodison (2005)

Good Morning and Good Night
David Wagoner (2005)

American Ghost Roses
Kevin Stein (2005)

National Poetry Series

Eroding Witness
Nathaniel Mackey (1985)
Selected by Michael S. Harper

Palladium
Alice Fulton (1986)
Selected by Mark Strand

Cities in Motion
Sylvia Moss (1987)
Selected by Derek Walcott

The Hand of God and a Few
Bright Flowers
William Olsen (1988)
Selected by David Wagoner

The Great Bird of Love
Paul Zimmer (1989)
Selected by William Stafford

Stubborn
Roland Flint (1990)
Selected by Dave Smith

The Surface
Laura Mullen (1991)
Selected by C. K. Williams

The Dig
Lynn Emanuel (1992)
Selected by Gerald Stern

My Alexandria
Mark Doty (1993)
Selected by Philip Levine

The High Road to Taos
Martin Edmunds (1994)
Selected by Donald Hall

Theater of Animals
Samn Stockwell (1995)
Selected by Louise Glück

The Broken World
Marcus Cafagña (1996)
Selected by Yusef Komunyakaa

Nine Skies
A. V. Christie (1997)
Selected by Sandra McPherson

Lost Wax
Heather Ramsdell (1998)
Selected by James Tate

So Often the Pitcher Goes to Water
until It Breaks
Rigoberto González (1999)
Selected by Ai

Renunciation
Corey Marks (2000)
Selected by Philip Levine

Manderley
Rebecca Wolff (2001)
Selected by Robert Pinsky

Theory of Devolution
David Groff (2002)
Selected by Mark Doty

Rhythm and Booze
Julie Kane (2003)
Selected by Maxine Kumin

Shiva's Drum
Stephen Cramer (2004)
Selected by Grace Schulman

Other Poetry Volumes

Local Men and *Domains*
James Whitehead (1987)

Her Soul beneath the Bone:
Women's Poetry on Breast Cancer
Edited by Leatrice Lifshitz (1988)

Days from a Dream Almanac
Dennis Tedlock (1990)

Working Classics:
Poems on Industrial Life
Edited by Peter Oresick and Nicholas Coles
(1990)

The University of Illinois Press
is a founding member of the
Association of American University Presses.

Composed in 11/14 Adobe Garamond
by Jim Proefrock
at the University of Illinois Press
Designed by Dennis Roberts
Manufactured by Thomson-Shore, Inc.

University of Illinois Press
1325 South Oak Street
Champaign, IL 61820-6903
www.press.uillinois.edu